FORGIVENESS FOR THE MAN'S SOUL

FORGIVENESS FOR THE MAN'S SOUL

Real Stories of Forgiveness and Faith

Alethea Pascascio

Queen Publications
Antioch, Illinois

www.queenpublications.com

We would like to acknowledge the many publishers and individuals who granted us permission to reprint the cited material. (Note: The stories that were written by Alethea Pascascio are not included in this listing.)

2006. Ghosts From Vietnam. Reprinted by permission of MSIA ©2006 by John-Roger (www.forgive.org). All rights reserved.

(Continued on page 140)

Library of Congress Cataloging-in-Publication Data

Forgiveness for the Man's Soul: Stories of Forgiveness and Faith / Alethea Pascascio
    p. cm.
    ISBN: 978-0-9778377-1-7
    1. Men- Antecdotes. 2. Women-Antecdotes. 3. Forgiveness-

LCCN: 2009906008

© 2009 Alethea Pascascio
ISBN: 978-0-9778377-1-7

All rights reserved. Printed in the United States of America. No part of this publication may be reproduced, stored in a retrieval system or transmitted in any form or by any means, electronic, mechanical, photocopying, recording or otherwise, without the written permission of the publisher.

Publisher: Queen Publications
        P.O. Box 496
        Antioch, IL 60002

Cover design & Inside formatting by Alethea Pascascio
Editor: Gregory Janicke

FORGIVENESS FOR THE MAN'S SOUL

Real Stories of Forgiveness and Faith

---

is presented to

---

by

---

date

---

occasion

Contents

Dedication..viii
Acknowledgments...ix
Share With Us..x
Foreword..xi
Introduction..xiii

1. ALL IN THE FAMILY

Given Up By Mama, Redeemed By God *Gilbert Palmer*......3
You Are Not The Father..8
Drinking And Not Thinking *J. Walsh*................................12
Standing On One Leg..16
Working Day And Night..22
The Child I Didn't Know-The Wife I Thought I Knew.....27
Being My Father's Keeper...31
Am I My Brother's Keeper..37

2. WHEN THE OUTSIDE COMES IN

The Ghosts of Vietnam..45
Living By The Sword *Harvey Jones* 48
Too Hungry To Hate *Roberto Garcia*................................54
Hurting Kids, Hurt Kids..59
The Truth Shall Set You Free..64
Not Very Neighborly...70
The Minister, My Wife and Me *M. Richards*......................75

3. FROM BEHIND PRISON WALLS

Adopted Twice *Briant George*..85
I Don't Hate God Anymore *John Miller*……....................105
Forgiven Sex Crime Offender *Robert Swift*.........................114
Being Able To Forgive Those I Hated... *Mark V*...................124

Prayer (A Gift To You)...133
Simple Steps to Forgiveness...134
More Forgiveness For The Soul? 136
Contributors..137
Discussion Questions...139

Permissions (*continued*) 140
Who Is Alethea Pascascio? 141

Dedication

-To every individual who is, has been, or will be plagued by the ills of unforgiveness.

Acknowledgments

To my Lord and Savior Jesus Christ who is the strength of my life and waaay better than good to me. Thank you for your love, faithfulness, grace, and mercy- and for dropping the seed of this book within my spirit. I know it will accomplish your divine purpose.

To my children, Alexis and Alaina, who have been my loudest cheerleaders. Thank you for your love, unwavering support, and all that you do to encourage me in my endeavors. I love all of you so much.

To my parents, Ray and Margaret Sherls, who love me unconditionally. Thank you for your encouraging words of wisdom and always supporting my visions.

To Apostle E. James and Pastor Deborah Logan, my family's Pastors and spiritual parents. Thank you for keeping your ears to heaven and obeying the voice of God. You have been the catalyst for needed change in my life and without you my spiritual muscles would be grossly underdeveloped. May God's Hand of wisdom, favor, power, and protection continue to rest upon your entire family.

To the entire Christian Faith Fellowship Zion church. Thank you for lovingly embracing our family and for your well wishes, thoughtfulness, and prayers. You truly are the Church of The Acts.

Share With Us

We would like to invite you to send stories you would like to see published in future editions of *Forgiveness for the Soul*.

We would also love to hear your reactions to the stories in this book. Please let us know what your favorite stories are and how they affected you.

Please send submissions to:

> Queen Publications
> *Forgiveness for the Soul*
> P.O. Box 496
> Antioch, IL 60002
> Email: forgiveness@queenpublications.com

You can also visit our website at:
www.queenpublications.com

We hope you enjoy reading this book as much as we enjoyed compiling, editing and writing it.

Foreword

I have had the pleasure of pastoring the Pascascio family and watching them grow in God's grace and knowledge. Their children are happy, healthy and interact well with others; this is a sign of children who are nurtured in an environment of love, correction and forgiveness.

We all need correction in order to understand life has boundaries. We all need forgiveness to understand when we cross those boundaries there are consequences, but these consequences do not include expulsion from the human race. We are still people made in the image and likeness of God with a future and a hope.

I've said over the pulpit, "Forgiveness is the one thing believers do that is most like God." I strongly believe this; God forgives more sins each day than probably anything else! Forgiveness is a divine attribute of God and as Christians we too must strive to constantly forgive.

When we fail to forgive we hold ourselves and those who hurt us prisoners in our hearts; prisoners who have been denied the freedom to continue a life with purpose. We actually become stuck in the moment! When we forgive we release ourselves and those who hurt us to continue a life with purpose free from the pain of the past.

To *for-give* is to literally give grace before it's needed! Jesus did this while in pain on the cross; He forgave us before we asked for it—what love! He said.. "Father forgive them for they know not what they do!"

To forgive is to release, let go and send away the offense.

As you read this book think of all the times God has forgiven you and will forgive you! Think of His endless mercy toward you when you crossed boundaries set by His Word—yet He kindly forgave and released you.

I pray you will not only see how God has released you but that you will also see the need to release those who hurt you.

Apostle E. James Logan
Senior Pastor Christian Faith Fellowship Church Zion
Destiny International Fellowship

Introduction

World news has become a flood threatening to engulf us: war, disease, terrorism, violence, spilling over from newspaper to TV to radio to Internet blogs. Add billions of heated opinions, and the tidal wave of conflict threatens to overwhelm us completely.

World weary, we start to fall into two camps: victim and survivor. We either suffer pain and loss or somehow struggle through it all, thanking God at the end of the day that nothing bad happened to us.

Consider Jonah, the man who wound up nearly drowning only to find himself in the belly of an exceptionally large fish. He lived in a world of war, disease, terrorism and violence. Jonah's job was to go to his most hated enemy – the Assyrians in Nineveh –and invite them to repent and seek forgiveness from the Lord God. Jonah was not the bravest of men, nor did he immediately rise above his hatred of Assyrians. Instead of confronting the enemy, he ran.

Jonah, servant of God, did not want to share his God with his enemy; instead, he booked passage on a ship heading in the opposite direction.

God brought forth a storm, overwhelming the ship. Jonah knew his betrayal was the cause, so he told the crew to throw him overboard. Reluctantly, begging God's forgiveness, the men did so and the sea grew calm.

A creature described in the Bible as a "large fish" then swallows Jonah whole. He is inside the fish for three days and three nights.

Consider this. He is lost in a sea. He sinks into desperate darkness. There is no light, no hope. What does Jonah do? Feel sorry for himself? Try to rationalize his decision to avoid the Assyrians? Complain?

No, he prays.

"In my distress, I called to the Lord, and he answered me. From the depths of my grave I called for help, and You listened to my cry" (Jonah 2:1). In his prayer, Jonah discovers the healing power of God's forgiveness. God frees Jonah from the fish. Jonah abides in the Lord's directive and speaks to the enemy, the people of Nineveh. They listen and repent.

You will read the stories of several modern men. Each underwent a difficult trial in life. Like Jonah, each finds himself lost in a sea, overwhelmed. Like Jonah, each finds healing and transformation.

Do you have a desire to forgive, and to be forgiven?

Start by accepting the invitation to Jesus Christ.

The road to forgiveness and healing begins with this first small step. Take it.

1

ALL IN THE FAMILY

*Forgiveness is the fragrance that
the violet sheds on the heel that has crushed it.*
Mark Twain

FEATURE:

Given Up By Mama, Redeemed By God
(The Gilbert Palmer Story)

My mother was a teen aged mother who made a lot of mistakes (who hasn't) coupled with raising a son during the civil rights era, a time period when many people of color suffered from all forms of abuse.

Abuse on any level is destructive in nature. The very word itself conjures pain, agony, over indulgence, broken relationships/separation leading to both physical and mental scaring and in some cases death. …leaving an indelible mark that can last a life-time and dictate how you respond to and treat others for years to come.

After learning of the importance of having the ability to forgive and forgive from the heart, I realized it was something, that if not already built in…you'd have to learn how to do.

I speak from a learned stand point. Coming from a dysfunctional family unit (and who hasn't- I once heard a man say that 'dysfunction' means "dis is how we function) …I had the will power and the desire to break the vicious cycle. My first personal relationship....

My mother (oldest of 9 children) at the age of 13 gave birth to a real live baby-doll…(that's what my aunts, all younger than my mother, thought I was) not knowing that this was going to require parental skills which she lacked.

My grandmother took the place of my mother and raised me as her own. My mother thought it was a good idea during the early years but as she got older she needed more ways to make ends meet so Food Stamps and Cash assistance was her answer…but she needed a child to claim. Used and abused that's what I became. Verbal and Sexual abuse by your mother is embarrassing…take it from me.

Therefore, looking at her day in and day out was torture during the late 60's and early 70's. I would literally wish her dead. My prayers would include, "God just kill her." I know now that.... She may not have realized how

ALL IN THE FAMILY

much she hurt me while living her life.

The one thing she did was buy me all kinds of books. I could only watch limited amounts of TV, so my world became my books. I recall having a series from Time-Life called "Man, Myth & Magic" of which I'd read about spells you can cast on people…and yes I tried them all- but nothing seemed to work.

It was during the mid 70's that she once again wanted to get rid of me so she falsified documents to send me off to the military. It was during my processing that they pulled me from line and asked me about the false document. I cried because I was embarrassed to tell the recruiter that my mom didn't want me anymore. Even the recruiter cried and gave me a ride to my grandmother's house. I lived there until I graduated from high school and etched a life for myself.

Many years went by and we became closer. I moved to another state 2000 miles away…time takes it's toll and sickness enters and God's Will be done… and in the middle of all that there was still the need for something to fill the hole in my life…..everyday.

Now that my mother is in a better place, the very

One who went to prepare the Place has Forgiven her (and us all)...So I promise to forgive all...every chance I get.

It has taken me a long time to realize and fully understand that the very best thing I can do for me, my children and for my mother is forgiveness. I was hurt yes… but -- I have become a better person for it.

In the bible I'm reminded that "My Happiness is in the LORD!" It is through Him that I can be happy. It is also through Him that I can forgive. He gives the ultimate picture of forgiveness in sending his Son to die on the cross for the sins of the world.

I have released the anger that I've held. I couldn't hold on to it any longer. It was not healthy. It did not make me happy. It did not strengthen me in any other aspect of my life. The anger I have felt only hindered me from moving on from that time in my life. I forgave her for everything. I asked her to forgive me as well.

Here is some of what I said to my ailing mother, one day, before I left her bedside, "You are forgiven for trying to find your way in life. You are forgiven for the many mistakes you've made. You are forgiven and there is nothing for you to do. Let the past be gone and all its stories too. And even as the stories come they will go again because you are forgiven forever."

She smiled with her heart and kissed me on the forehead.

You Are Not The Father

Faith is the rock that stands the test of any storm. After the storm, there is light.

In this story, a man finds his faith tested in a shocking way. The true test of a man is how he responds to disturbing situations. In times of trial, do you let hostility and bitterness rule your life? Does your faith stand fast against the storm?

How can your life improve through forgiveness? How can the word of God in the Bible change you for good, forever? Consider these questions as you read. Consider these questions as you take your next steps in life.

If you wonder about certain behavior or activities, ask yourself: What would Jesus do? Then find the answer to that question in the Bible. The answers are there, waiting for you, waiting to change you. Read Matthew, Mark, Luke

ALL IN THE FAMILY

and John and discover how the life of Jesus Christ can help your life today.

***

My wife and I were pillars of our community. We were active in church and served as administrators in the local educational system. Our only son was the apple of my eye. He wanted so much to be like me and I wanted him to as well. He even copied my walk.

As soon as 'David' graduated from high school and left for college, my wife of 19 years started getting antsy.

Within months, she started talking of leaving me to pursue her own happiness since our only child had left the nest. Then she proceeded to tell me that she was leaving me for 'David's' real father. I came to find out my wife had had a long-distance affair over the course of 18 years.

I walked around for months in a comatose state, then finally snapped out of it and filed for divorce. We both told our son and a DNA test proved I indeed wasn't his biological father. No sooner than the divorce was final, my ex-wife's relationship with her lover ended and she wanted to return to me. I didn't take her back.

I was bitter and distrusting of women for the next three years. Then without knowing it, I allowed a woman to slip under the walls I'd built. On the verge of losing out on a wonderful relationship with an awesome woman, I chose to stand on my faith and take one day at a time to start a new beginning.

Faith means believing in something you can't see. While I professed having faith throughout my life, I really felt it being put to the test. Did I trust in God as much as I said I did? Where would I start?

Prayer, of course. But sometimes the words just aren't there. I needed more than what my mind could tell me. I turned to God's word and listened, really listened.

What did Jesus say while on the cross? Did He shower the people with hatred? He asked God the Father to forgive them.

Forgiveness.

The answer to prayer. The new beginning for me.

My relationship with this new woman took off after I called my ex-wife and told her I forgave her for the years of disrespect, dishonesty, and disregard. Then I forgave myself for missing out on life for three years. Through

ALL IN THE FAMILY

faith, I took responsibility for my actions, for my present and future.

My son still hasn't built a relationship with his biological father, yet our relationship is closer than ever.

***

PRAYER: Father, when your Son was upon the cross, dying for our sins, He called out to You and asked You to forgive everyone. Not just one or two people, but everyone. Help me learn how to forgive, with compassion. Help me model my life on Jesus and unlock the deep faith residing in my heart. When times get hard, the strong look to you, Lord, to Your wisdom and counsel. You are faithful to us, as we must be to you.

Open the eyes of my heart Lord. I do want to see You. Amen.

Drinking And Not Thinking

Only God is in control of all things – from the great constellations in the heavens to the smallest creature on earth. He is everywhere. He knows everything. Nothing we do remains hidden.

In this story, one choice leads to another until a situation falls out of control. How should the man in the story have acted? What does he decide to do? What would you do in a similar situation?

We always seem to have answers about how other people should live their lives or the mistakes they have made. How do you live your own life? What guidelines do you use?

A human life doesn't come with an owner's manual – or does it? The Bible is a blueprint for learning how to live. Life isn't always easy –but forgiveness and rebirth are as close as the pages of God's Holy Word.

ALL IN THE FAMILY

***

I was taught that drinking wasn't good but believed that was an exaggeration when it came to having a glass of wine socially. Then the day came when the babysitter stopped over and cried on my shoulder while my wife of eight years was at work. To help her calm down, I offered her a glass of red wine.

She began explaining how she was about to get evicted from her apartment and might be in the danger of losing her car. I told her I would talk to my wife about getting her a pay advance if that would help her situation. Still drinking wine, we discussed how to avoid these financial problems in the future.

Somehow, this conversation led into a discussion about her love life or lack thereof.

Then the compliments started. She appeared to be my biggest fan, telling me what a great father and provider I was. How handsome I was. How she desired a man like me. How she was jealous when she saw me holding my wife's hand or heard me saying that I loved her. This conversation went on for almost an hour. Before I knew it, I (45 years old) was massaging her neck while she (28 years old) giggled.

The massage led to kissing, which led to nothing because my wife walked in without either of us hearing her enter through the door. Through a lot of yelling, tears, and words I can't repeat, I tried to explain to my wife how my ego and the wine got the best of me.

It would take almost two years for our marriage to make it through this. And even though I asked God for forgiveness the evening it happened, I still was down on myself for months. It was almost a year before my wife said she forgave me.

Our child had to get to know another nanny and basically start all over -- my fault.

My wife thought we had been having an illicit affair behind her back and that our evening had been planned out -- this too was my fault.

After two years of being fully accountable- every day- for all of my actions, I finally feel a sense of restoration and believe the incident actually opened up the lines of communication.

***

PRAYER: Dear Lord, we find it easy to blame other

ALL IN THE FAMILY

people for the way we act, for the choices we make. We act upon impulse, we stumble in our weakness. But let us look to you for strength. You are a rock, Lord, against all trials in life. You are a rock and our salvation. Lord, lift my heart on high, turn my eyes toward You so that I may stay focused on your heavenly inspiration.

Forgive me, Lord. Heal me. Help me find a sense of restoration in Your Holy Word, the Bible. Let me seek and find new meaning, both in the Bible and in my life. Let the words and actions of Jesus guide me in my day-to-day life. Amen.

Standing On One Leg

The Book of Proverbs in the Bible serves as a priceless guide to moral truth. It tells us in numerous ways how to resist temptation, speak openly and honestly, live in faith and grow in wisdom through God's Holy Words. Proverbs, written by the wise King Solomon, reaches through the ages to touch our minds and hearts in the 21st century. The words of ancient times ring true in this very moment.

Proverbs 3 tells us, "Trust in the Lord with all your heart and lean not on your own understanding; in all your ways acknowledge Him, and He will make your paths straight. Do not be wise in your own eyes; fear the Lord and shun evil. This will bring health to your body and nourishment to your bones" (Proverbs 3:5-8).

When we feel temptations, we must strive to give our lives to the Lord. When our good sense crumbles to wrong decisions, we need to hear the voice of God in our

ALL IN THE FAMILY

souls. When we give in to anger and rage, we must cling to the message of the Holy Bible as never before.

Read the following story and consider the choices of the husband and wife. In one split second, the unbelievable happens and a life changes forever.

What are the possible results of life's great trials? Can forgiveness and healing exist? Can we continue to acknowledge the Lord in all our ways?

***

A wrong decision led to the worst night of my life.

It was late, and I wanted a distraction, some excitement. I should have stayed home, but I didn't. I wanted to get out. Against my wife's wishes, I took off with some unsavory associates to what is sometimes called a "Gentleman's Club." There I was, a Christian man making a very bad decision.

Why wasn't I listening to the words of my faith? I was weak. I gave in to temptation. I rationalized that I wasn't doing anything wrong, not really. I wasn't hurting anybody.

Things got a lot worse before they got better. I didn't have a good time knowing I would have to deal with my wife's anger when I returned home.

After finally dragging my friends out of the club, I returned home at 3 a.m. I felt guilty for having patronized such an establishment. It was the wrong thing to do, and I knew it. I asked God for His forgiveness as I tried to put my key into the door. I tried again and again, but it soon became obvious that the locks had been changed.

I knocked with great force on the door three times, then I felt a blast come through the door and knock me onto my back. Time seemed to stand still as I felt the worst pain ever travel up my thigh.

I reached down to touch my knee and felt warmth. I passed out. I came to hours later in the emergency room of the local hospital. What was happening? Was I having a nightmare? One minute, I was coming home. The next minute, I was on my back, in a strange room with bright lights. It didn't make sense. It was all unreal – except for the pain. The incredible burning pain that would not go away.

I was confused, maybe delirious. I didn't know what was up or down. I nearly fainted again when the doctor came in and told me that my wife had shot through

ALL IN THE FAMILY

the door and had shot my right leg off from below the knee.

Was the doctor talking to me? The words didn't make any sense. This had to be happening to someone else, not me.

I thanked the Lord that I survived that night, that the blast had not gone through my chest. I was living a nightmare, but at least I was still alive. Waves of anger went through me. Why? Why had she done this? I wasn't hurting anyone going to that club……or was I? Was I hurting myself and my wife? I claimed to be a Christian man, a follower of Jesus. That meant I believed His words and lived them out every way, every day. Jesus doesn't want half-followers, people who say they believe in Him but do what they want.

Slowly, gradually, as the world settled and started to make a little sense again, I felt grateful to be alive.

The doctor took care of me, but I had to have a prosthesis.

I had yet another shock that night. My wife appeared in the doorway of my hospital room. She was the last person I expected to see. Her eyes were red with tears. She came to me and fell across the bed sobbing saying that she thought I was someone trying to break into the house.

What was I to do? Should I reject her? Use my anger against her? My mind whirled. My heart pounded.

Would this be the end of us?

The final shock came from what I did next. Before I knew it, I had placed my hand on my wife's back and whispered three words. "I forgive you."

Somehow, it wasn't me talking. It was the spirit of the Lord in me that formed the words. Forgiveness, true forgiveness, soon brought healing to both of us.

***

PRAYER: Dear Lord, You know that our lives can be filled with confusion, temptation, pain, hatred and sorrow. You tend to us in thousands of unseen ways. Thank You for the protection you provide us, your humble servants.

Let us live according to Your Holy Word, with each day, each moment dedicated to You. In this way, our direction is clear. We do not waste a single minute. We open our eyes and focus on You, on heaven.

As we focus on heaven, let pain and sorrow fall by

the wayside, let repentance and forgiveness fill our lives like a healing breeze, let the love You show for us resound across the earth in a chorus of thanksgiving. This we ask in Your Name. Amen.

Working Day And Night

Sometimes a father can say as much with his silence and absence as he can with his words. In these times, the Christian man must step up and offer forgiveness to his father, then seek forgiveness for his own similar actions.

The Lord desires peace and harmony for all. Read the following story and see how the two men come to terms with their differences. Is there someone in your life with whom you need to reconcile? Is there a son or daughter crying out for your loving attention?

The Bible clearly states, "Fathers, do not exasperate your children; instead, bring them up in the training and instruction of the Lord" (Ephesians 6:1).

***

"Mama, is Daddy coming home early today?"

Even as a grown man, I can stand and look out the window of my Manhattan-area corner office and hear those words echoing in my mind. That question had haunted me

ALL IN THE FAMILY

since I was a child. I always hoped my father would simply come home from work on time, and laugh and play with me. I hoped that he would give me the love and attention any child needed and deserved. I hoped, day after day.

My father worked non-stop. He never did come home when I thought he would. He never gave me the time and love I wanted. Eventually this caused my parents to separate and I saw him even less.

You would think his behavior would make me stay at home a lot with my children. Instead, like my father, I worked non-stop. For years I thought I was just an overachiever. There was no way I would neglect my children.

The truth was that it didn't matter if it was my children, wife or friends, I wouldn't take off of work for much of anything or anyone. Except my father. If he came in town, all bets were off. I felt like a kid trying to impress Dad every time I brought him to my office and showed him the skyline. Then I'd take him to my home and show him my idea of what a real family should look like and how they should act and how the Dad is supposed to be present to love his kids. Problem was, if he wasn't in town visiting me, I wouldn't have been at home doing any of that.

During his last visit, my wife had to tell him everything about the kids because I hadn't been at home enough to know much. I felt horrible and for once realized that I had spent too much time trying to feel good and worthy enough to have my Dad's love.

After my parents divorced, my Dad and I were supposed to have scheduled visits, but he hardly ever came to pick me up. To my kid brain, his actions meant that he did not love me. So year after year, I was driven by my disappointment in him and in myself for not being the child who was interesting enough or good enough to have his father be active in his life. This lasted until I was 38 years old and feeling 83. I was exhausted. So while Dad was visiting us, I decided that it was finally time to put all of the cards on the table.

As I dropped him off at the airport, I said, "Dad, I forgive you for my childhood disappointments and let-downs. It's been controlling me to the point where I've been neglecting my own children to impress you."

My Dad and I talked for several minutes. He explained what happened back then, apologized, and cried.

Well, okay, we both cried. He opened his heart to

ALL IN THE FAMILY

me and revealed what his own burdens had been for so long. It was as if we had been standing on opposite sides of a big brick wall for years. Finally, we tore down the wall between us.

Instead of resenting my father, I could now respect him. I could see life as he saw it. I could reveal my own pains and regrets, and begin to heal. It had seemed nearly impossible to ever reach out to my father. I'm glad I did.

Time has passed, and I am a much better father today. I even coach my children's soccer team. Time moves quickly. They will only be children once. I'll be their dad forever.

***

PRAYER: Dear Heavenly Father, you sent your Son, Jesus Christ, to us to redeem us of our sins. You once said, "This is My Beloved Son, in Whom I am well pleased." Let us give thanks for God the Father and for our fathers on earth, silent or absent though they may be. Let us have the courage and conviction to overcome our anger, our doubts and seek the relationship you had with Your Divine Son.

Let us walk prayerfully. Let us forgive our fathers'

transgressions, if need be, let us forgive our own shortcomings and come to you for guidance, inspiration and love. Show us the way to kindness and responsible behavior. This we ask in Your Name. Amen.

The Child I Didn't Know: The Wife I Thought I Knew

How well do we know someone – a family member, a spouse? The man in this story makes a shocking discovery after 20 years of marriage.

As you read this story, consider how you might feel in the same situation. What would your reactions be? We can learn from others just how charitable – or unkind – we can be. What are our options?

In the Book of Nahum in the Old Testament, we discover that "The Lord is slow to anger and great in power" (Nahum1:3). "The Lord is good, a refuge in times of trouble, He cares for those who trust in Him" (Nahum 1:7). Are we quick to anger? Do we seek shelter with the Lord in times of trouble? When our faith is tested, do we reject Him or accept His love and compassion?

***

Twenty years of marriage and no children. I'm 52 years old now and so is my wife, so the possibility of an heir has gone out of the window. For the first five years of our marriage, we tried desperately for a child, but to no avail, at least that's what I thought.

We were in the process of selling our home and moving into something smaller due to the downturn in the economy. We've lived in the home for 19 years and had accumulated so much stuff that we decided to donate a lot of it. So, I went into the attic to remove the years of possessions we'd stowed away up there.

While pillaging through some things, I found a folder containing receipts, doctor's orders and other pieces of paper with my wife listed as the Patient. When it all came together, I realized I was looking at proof of an abortion during the second year of our marriage -- which was during the time we supposedly were trying to have a baby. I felt like someone had slit my throat and allowed all of my life to pour out.

It would take months, even years, to forgive this betrayal. I thought we were living on Christian values, yet there was the taking of a life, a lie, deception, betrayal.

ALL IN THE FAMILY

And as much as I wanted to hate my wife for taking away my legacy, our legacy, I couldn't do it. I had signed on for better or worse. And that moment was the worst for me.

I had no idea exactly what to do next. I was too focused on my own pain to really see beyond it. I came to realize that the Christian words I lived by had to truly mean something to me: love, trust, forgiveness, hope. They aren't just words written in a book – they had to be written on my heart also, with clear conviction.

I had always said that I believed in God. Did I really? Did I trust he would heal me? Heal my marriage?

I prayed and prayed.

I eventually confronted my wife. I found that, on some level, I was able to forgive her. This brought some relief. I truly thought we had moved on that day. But I wept whenever I saw people with their babies. Sometimes when you go to the well of pain and tears, it's even deeper than you can imagine.

Over the past four years, God has given me the peace to accept this thing that I could not change and to love my wife as He loves us -- unconditionally and despite our imperfections. This is truly a gift of life that I can embrace with an open heart.

***

PRAYER: Dear Lord, lead us from darkness in our times of need. Free us from anger and feelings of betrayal, help us to focus on how we can give greater glory to You in heaven through our actions here on earth. Our time here is short. Help us make each day count – for our families, friends, acquaintances and the strangers we might meet. Inspire us so that we can put our longings and talents to work for You. This we humbly ask in Your Name. Amen.

ALL IN THE FAMILY

Being My Father's Keeper

When life goes on from day to day, we can easily lull ourselves into a routine. We get up, eat breakfast, go to work, come home, watch TV and go to sleep. Then the cycle begins all over again.

Before we know it, years have passed in the same dull cycle. Sometimes it takes an illness or accident to snap us out of the cycle. We discover that we are mortal, that our family members are mortal and that the cycle won't go on forever. Suddenly every moment, every breath becomes important.

In the following story, a man tells of his abuse as a child, his misconceived choices in life and his journey to redemption. His journey begins and ends with his father.

***

My childhood was not one you would say was normal and wholesome. It was the opposite. My father abused my mother, my little sister and me. My mother is now deceased and my sister lives with her husband in England, where she happily pretends that our father is no longer a part of her life.

I, on the other hand, went through a stint with drug and alcohol abuse, trying to escape the past and feel some sense of worth. This went on for waaaaay too long. After finally getting tired of myself, I slowly let go of the addictions and managed to maintain a distant relationship with my father. It wasn't warm and loving, but it was the best I could do then. It was better than nothing.

Time passed. When my father was 76, he had a stroke that left him incapacitated. There was no one to call but me. I was 36.

I had mixed feelings about seeing him in the hospital. It was not easy. I could not forget the past. I could not forget what he had done to me, to my mother, to my sister. How could I? It had affected my whole life.

As I rode to the hospital, I braced myself. I didn't know what to expect. I felt so many conflicting emotions. Nothing seemed clear.

When I walked into the hospital, I was startled. I saw a shadow of the man I feared so greatly while growing up. My father was tired and weak and small. He could barely move. He was completely at my mercy and needed someone to care for him and ensure that the hospital gave him their best medical attention.

Suddenly, everything was different. My whole world changed. I was the tall, independent person in charge of the situation. My father was small and helpless, like a child.

We looked at each other. We both knew that the tides had turned. The question was what would happen next. We did some awkward small talk that meant nothing. After the years of silence, it was almost impossible to bridge that gap with words of any meaning.

Time went by slowly in the hospital room. I really didn't know what was going to happen. We might have made a little more small talk; I might have gone my way.

After a silence that seemed to last for eternity, my father spoke. He said, "Now you can do whatever you want to me. All of the ways you imagined hurting me. Now you have the power."

It was not what I expected him to say. To be honest, I thought about it and considered disconnecting his oxygen.

I was in a position to get even with him for all the pain he had caused me in life. His weakness put me in a position of strength. Now he knew how I had felt those many years ago.

And I could have walked away. I *wanted* to walk away. If he died from the stroke, then our relationship would be over, once and for all. I would have nothing to do with him anymore.

I looked at him. He gazed up at me. In the quiet of the room, I considered my revenge. Then something outside my anger came to me. It might have been a thought. Or a feeling. Or something from my soul.

If I walked away, if I ignored my father now in his time of greatest need, that would make me just like him. I would be just like the man I had hated all my life. How could I live with myself that way? I would be continuing in the same cycle of anger and regret I had lived with for so much of my life. Ignoring my father in his time of need – or, even worse, walking away from him – would not break the cycle. It would only continue it in ways I couldn't even imagine.

"Now you have the power," he had said to me. He

ALL IN THE FAMILY

had surrendered to me.

I summoned what courage I had. I carefully considered my words then said, "No, Dad, I forgive you for all of the hurt and pain you caused me. And I am going to help you through this." I wasn't sure where that came from.

And as hard as it was to speak, my words did not throw open a door of emotion like you see in the movies. I'm not sure I really forgave my father that day as much as I needed to, but it definitely was a beginning.

I couldn't erase decades of time in one moment, in a couple of sentences.

There was light, though, in all the darkness. Maybe my father and I could start all over again. It was worth a try.

I eventually put action to my words. Nothing happened overnight, but our relationship improved, little by little. I took care of my father for the next six years until he passed away. We grew to become the best father and son team you could ever imagine. I only wish we could have become that way much earlier in life before his illness.

***

PRAYER: Dear Lord, You are in every moment, in every breath. Let us remember You well throughout the day. Let our thoughts and actions become a living prayer, full of repentance, forgiveness, hope and love.

It is a supreme challenge to forget the sins of the past and move on, but we must. We must move on and follow Jesus to our heavenly reward. We pray for our parents, our brothers and sisters, our children, all those whose lives we touch. May we pray and change and become shining examples of Your Word. The task often seems impossible; yet it is not.

Lift us when we are down, guide us when we stray, offer us comfort when we are weak. We come to you with contrite hearts. Help us, Lord. This we ask in Your name. Amen.

Am I My Brother's Keeper

"Am I my brother's keeper?" (Genesis 4:9)

Troubles and rivalries between brothers goes as far back as the Book of Genesis in the Bible, when Cain killed his brother, Abel, out of jealousy and anger. When God asks Cain where Abel is, he utters the dark question about being his "brother's keeper" in sheer defiance of the Lord. The Lord, in turn, condemns Cain and says to him, "You will be a restless wanderer on the earth" (Genesis 4:12).

Are we wanderers upon the earth, going from one situation to the next without feeling any spiritual satisfaction? What can we do to find peace, love and understanding?

The Book of Proverbs is a rich treasure, full of wisdom and compassion. It offers unprecedented insights into human nature, guiding us away from evil and harm toward God's holy light.

"For the Lord gives wisdom, and from His mouth

come knowledge and understanding. He holds victory in store for the upright, He is a shield to those whose walk is blameless, for He guards the course of the just and protects the way of His faithful ones" (Proverbs 2:6).

Proverbs continues to express the following: "The path of the righteous is like the first gleam of dawn, shining ever brighter 'til the full light of day" (Proverbs 4:18).

May the first gleaming of dawn shine upon your life.

***

My brother went through a tough divorce and was without a place to call home. I let him move in with me. Six months after his arrival, a check was missing from my checkbook and $7,000 missing out of my bank account. It had taken me quite a while to save this money to pay my real estate taxes.

After several days, I finally confronted my brother. After many lies, he finally admitted to stealing the money and paying off some of his gambling debts. I've known my brother all of his life and that is the first time I had heard of him having a gambling problem.

Although he had nowhere to go, I still asked him to

ALL IN THE FAMILY

move out of my home. I could not trust him. Now the tax bill was due and I had no way of coming up with another $7,000. Because of this I eventually had to sell my house.

I did not speak to my brother for two years.

Then I landed a good-paying job and was able to purchase another home. This house was better than the one I had lost. That's how the Lord works. We think we know it all, but He has a plan for us. A better plan than we can imagine. It's not just improving our lot in life, getting one house that's better than the last. It's abiding in His Word and learning that the best is yet to come, if we believe and practice our faith.

I had ignored my brother for two years, but then something amazing happened. The Lord was working within me. I couldn't put my finger on the exact moment, but after a while I knew that God had a plan for me, and it was good. I had a conversation with a family member who told me my brother was trying to purchase his first home. I began to think about him and miss him. *Really* miss him.

The pain, mistrust and anger that had covered my heart seemed to fall away. God's Divine Light filled my heart and soul with new meaning. The "past" was something said and done and best forgotten. It was my present behavior, and my future with my brother, that counted. Life is too short to waste any time harboring grudges against one's brother.

After much thought and prayer, I contacted my brother. We reconnected in ways I never thought possible. I forgave him for what he did to me those years ago. Somehow, forgiveness broke down the barrier between us. The Lord was true to us.

When I forgave my brother, it wasn't just talk. I also gave him $5,000 for a down-payment on his new home. I wanted us all to start a new life, thanks be to God.

***

PRAYER: Dear Heavenly Father, guide us through our days. Show us that while life here is temporary, life with You in heaven is eternal. We must prepare ourselves now.

You said, "Lend to them without expecting to get anything back. Then your reward will be great" (Luke 6:35). Let us open our eyes to You, Lord, let us hear Your Word, let us act with love and understanding. Then our

ALL IN THE FAMILY

reward will be great. We will be one with You.

Help us join with our brothers in glorious praise of your Holy Name. Amen.

ALL IN THE FAMILY

2

WHEN THE OUTSIDE COMES IN

They who forgive most, shall be most forgiven.

Josiah Bailey

FEATURE:
The Ghosts of Vietnam

If you've seen any pictures of the Vietnam War, you've probably seen this picture. A 9 year old Vietnamese girl, her clothes burned off by napalm, is fleeing an American-led assault on her village. She is running toward the camera, her mouth open wide in terror and incomprehensible pain.

For John Plummer, that picture is forever a part of him. He was the American chopper pilot responsible for raining fire that day on the village of Trang.

The next day when that picture hit the front pages, John Plummer was devastated by it. For 24 years he carried the image of that burned and terrified girl in his mind.

Three marriages, two divorces, a severe drinking problem - and then the TV newscast that night that showed that girl's picture again - and then showed that woman today, now living in Toronto.

That was the first John Plummer even knew the girl who had haunted his conscience for so long was still alive. He learned her name was Kim Phuc, now 33 years old. He watched and saw the thick white scars the splashing napalm had left on her neck and arm and back. He learned she had 17 operations but still lives with pain.

Not long before, John's long struggle led him to surrender his life to God. And now he wanted to face Kim. Providentially, he got that opportunity at a Veterans Day observance at the Vietnam War Memorial. Kim was the speaker.

When she finished, John Plummer fought his way through the crowd to try to reach her. He did. This time, there was no news photographer to take the picture - but it was an unforgettable moment. John told Kim who he was and she just opened her arms to him. He fell into her arms sobbing. All he could say was, "I'm so sorry. I'm just so sorry." And the woman with the scars from what he had done patted his back and said these words, "It's all right. I forgive. I forgive."

WHEN THE OUTSIDE COMES IN 47

Those are two words that you may need to hear. From the one you have hurt the most. From the One who bears the scars of what you did. The words - "I forgive." We've all done things we're not proud of - things we wish we could erase from our conscience. We know it's called sin. And though there may not be a photograph to haunt us, we still carry the weight, the guilt, the regret of all those "sins". "I forgive." Those words are not cheap, it has the power to chase away all the hates. It can make enemies become friends again... Most of all, it turns hate to love.

Living By The Sword
(Harvey Jones)

"The Lord is my rock, my fortress and my deliverer; my God is my rock in whom I take refuge. He is my shield and the horn of my salvation, my stronghold. I call to the Lord, who is worthy of praise, and I am saved from my enemies" (Psalm 18:1-3).

At times, forgiveness seems impossible. The pain of life bears down like a heavy boulder, crushing our hope. We suffer from abandonment. Our lives tumble down a path, away from the shelter of the Lord. We suffer at the hand of enemies. We cry out for revenge.

In darkest hours, in the toughest of times, the Lord stands by us to lift us from despair. He is our refuge against the storm, our light in the darkness. "As for God, His way is perfect; the word of the Lord is flawless. He is a shield for all who take refuge in him" (Psalm 18: 30).

In the following story, pain and a desire for revenge lead in a surprising way to the light of forgiveness.

***

"Live by the sword, die by the sword." That's a creed known by people who work in fields that are not legal or safe.

It didn't start out that way for me. I had my eyes on a career in science, maybe even becoming a doctor. I was always good in biology. Got straight A's.

Then my father left the family for another woman and I had to drop out of school and help out the family by getting a part-time job. Then before I knew it, I was helping a local drug dealer by making drops (runs) for him.

Something like that made me thousands of dollars a week. After a couple of years, I met my wife, had a kid and moved up in the organization enough to have my own runners.

Sure, I did and had a lot of people do things I'm not proud of, but I never thought it would all come back on me so fast. I'd been in the drug game for eight years, and thought all was going well for me. To make a long story short, I had made some enemies and they decided to get me where it would hurt the most. They caught my wife and child alone. Both of them were beat and tortured in ways I don't even want to describe.

The police knew it was a drug-infested community so they didn't do much. It would take several months for my wife and kid to heal externally. And once they were well enough to travel, my wife took my daughter and left me for good.

I had already made it my life's mission to hunt down those responsible and kill them. But once my family left me, my mission became an obsession. Problem was I had too many enemies and everybody was being tightlipped about who did it.

I slowly got out of the *game* and got into some legitimate businesses but lived in my own personal hell for years. I even blamed my father for the bad decisions I had made. I hated him and wanted him dead too. Yep, blamed everybody but myself.

Then I went to the prison to visit one of my friends from back in my drug-dealing days. I expected us to talk about old times, but he started talking about how he had joined a Bible study class. At first, I had no idea what he meant. He said that so many men were in prison because of forgiveness problems and that the answers to all problems

WHEN THE OUTSIDE COMES IN   51

were in God's Holy Word.

At first, I wanted to ignore him, but then I became intrigued. Something inside of me told me to keep listening. Although I pretended as if I wasn't interested, I wanted to learn more about forgiveness and the healing power of the Bible.

My friend had come to a realization that he had to forgive the man who had tried to rob him so he wouldn't get out and try to hurt the man. I kept feigning to be disengaged until I saw the seriousness in his face. Normally, he wasn't serious about very much. Now he was talking to me about the Bible and how his life had changed as if I was a member of the parole board.

Over the years we had several visits. I don't know when, but his words started to sink in.

Four years passed. Someone called and revealed to me who had hurt my family and where they could be found. I ran out of the door, jumped in the car and pulled up at the park where they were having a picnic with their families. I sat and watched and heard my friend's voice – all the way from prison. *Forgive. Forgive. Forgive.*

I said, "God, if this forgiveness stuff is real, show

me. Otherwise, I'm gonna kill these men and their families." I counted to ten, then reached for the door handle. My mother rang my cell phone and said my father was there and needed to talk to me.

Sounds strange, but he asked for my forgiveness for him leaving and causing me to drop out of school. I broke down crying and drove off.

God had intervened at a critical moment in my life. He had come to me in a time of my most desperate need. The "forgiveness stuff" was real.

It would take months, but I finally forgave myself, my Dad and the men who hurt my family. I left them alone, once and for all. My life got better and better.

God stood by me. Now I stand by Him.

***

PRAYER: We come before you, Lord, with heads bowed in humility and hands clasped in prayer. You free us from darkness and lead us to Your Light. Your prophet, Isaiah, said, "The people walking in darkness have seen a great light; on those living in the land of the shadow of death, a light has dawned" (Isaiah 9:2).

WHEN THE OUTSIDE COMES IN

We do not want to live in the shadow of death. We seek your eternal life. Lord, You are our Counselor, our Comforter, our Creator. Help us cleanse ourselves of the past. We want to forgive and be forgiven. Let us honor your creations, the men, woman and children of the world, with astonishing kindness and compassion.

Teach us to be amazing, to be shining examples of Your Divine Will. This we ask in Your Holy Name. Amen.

Too Hungry To Hate
(Roberto Garcia)

"Do to others as you would have them do to you" (Luke 6:31).

"Do not judge, and you will not be judged" (Luke 6:37).

Jesus shocked the world with His Words. He spoke in clear directives about love, faith, forgiveness, harmony.

According to Jesus, it is not for us to judge another people or treat them unfairly. Somehow, though, we do it all the time. Think of the words people use when others cut them off in line at the store or on a highway during rush hour. Think of the times people judge each other simply based on the color of their skin.

History is full of judgment. People in the time of Jesus judged that He should die nailed to a cross. Jesus asked His Father to forgive everyone. He died and rose again on the third day, bringing salvation to all of

WHEN THE OUTSIDE COMES IN

humankind.

In the following story, people in a community rush to judgment. It takes a powerful act of nature and an even more powerful act of Christian forgiveness to transform the community into a place rich with kindness.

***

I came from Mexico and worked hard to have what you call the American dream. I work for a popular technology company, making decent money and felt I would be received as a productive member of society.

I moved into a predominately white community and immediately began to see that people didn't necessarily view me as I viewed myself. My next-door neighbor came over when I was moving in and greeted one of the white movers and asked him if any of the Mexican movers knew of someone who could landscape her yard. He laughed and pointed to me.

She came over to me and inquired about landscaping and I told her that once I had settled in to my new home, I would look through some of my business cards and find her one. Her mouth dropped. "So," she said, "you're the new owner, but how... I mean…" Then she stormed off.

She did everything from that moment on to make me feel unwelcome. Many others in the neighborhood followed her lead. One even told me to get back on the boat I came in on. While another told me, "*Y'all needs to speak English all of the time.*" I corrected his so-called perfect English. He became offended and spit on the ground in front of me.

A few months later, a storm came through the community and took down several power lines. I was the only one in the neighborhood with a generator. This was quite a powerful position to be in. For the first two days, I let my neighbors suffer. It's strange how people can't suffer (hot, hungry, thirsty, disgruntled, etc.) and be racist at the same time. They had left me alone and launched all their insults at the power company.

Then something turned inside of me – a change of heart, you might say. I saw my neighbors the way I wanted them to see me – as an ordinary person with a family, a job and a home. Our skin colors or accents might be different, but, down deep, we pretty much all wanted the same things

WHEN THE OUTSIDE COMES IN

for our families – food, water and safety.

It dawned on me that I needed to forgive the people living in the homes near me and down the street. I had to rise above my own defensiveness and hostility. I had to forgive.

In the Bible, forgiveness is everything. It seemed impossible to do what Jesus said and "turn the other cheek." He had said that over 2,000 years ago. What did that have to do with me and a storm and a power failure? How could I put His words into action?

The answer came clear. I decided to practice forgiveness by doing an act of kindness. It wasn't easy. I went to the neighbors who had treated me the worst and asked them if they needed to use the freezer, watch TV, wash clothes and do other simple things one usually took for granted. Something amazing happened. I could see so much ignorance melt away from them as their eyes lit up with gratitude.

I had no idea what I was setting in motion by being forgiving and kind, but it trickled throughout the neighborhood, which has caused us to form a very tightly knit community regardless of nationality. Kindness can be contagious. Jesus said thousands of years ago to do well to evil doers. His Words are still valuable today. Putting them into action changed a community. Communities can change the world.

***

PRAYER: Dear Lord, let me not rush to judgment. We are all Your children. You created the heavens, the earth, the millions of plants and animals, the billions of people upon the planet. You created us in all our diversity.

In a perfect world, we celebrate differences. As You know, Lord, this is not a perfect world. At times, we fail and fall, condemning strangers for their looks, their skin color, their accents. Let us look beyond the surface into the soul of a stranger. Let us find our similarities and celebrate our differences.

Let us look to you for guidance and inspiration. May we model our lives after Yours and live in peace and love. We ask this in Your Name. Amen.

Hurting Kids, Hurt Kids

The trials of life can come at any age, even in childhood. Actions by others can darken an innocent life, leaving that life broken.

The broken life can lead to anger and despair. The world of hope seems far and silent. Read the following story and learn how one man's life changes dramatically as he seeks trust and forgiveness in the Lord.

***

I never knew the innocent joy of childhood. My mother was on drugs most of my childhood and my father was killed by a stray bullet when I was six. Suddenly, I was a lonely child. Life without a family left me feeling empty and alone.

And three teenaged boys in my neighborhood took advantage of my loneliness. When I was 12 they introduced me to marijuana and gained my trust, which temporarily gave me a false sense of family and belonging.

Without my knowledge, the young men laced the marijuana with an unknown substance that caused me to pass out. After waking the next day, the soreness and discomfort could only mean that I had been sexually violated. Being a scared little boy, I confided in my mother with no results.

Over time, I found myself falling victim to those three boys again and again. It was not until one of the assaults caused internal damage that my mother finally took action. I was removed from the home and raised in foster care.

By the age of 17, I finally accepted the fact that these acts of violence had stirred homosexual tendencies. But, I didn't want to be homosexual, so I fought against it and, out of sheer desperation, tried to commit suicide. The attempt failed. I slowly, gradually came back from the edge of despair. I chose celibacy. By the age of 25, I had been celibate for six years.

One day, I decided to go to church with a coworker for the first time in my life. It was Mother's Day, a day that can be charged with sad emotion or filled with gratitude. In

WHEN THE OUTSIDE COMES IN

my case, I thought it was the worse day of the year yet I still went on to church anyway.

In the quiet sanctity of church, I listened carefully to God's message. I did not only listen with my ears. I listened with my heart.

There were no quick and easy answers in church on a day honoring mothers. There was a mountain of hatred and rage for me to overcome. I knew, though, not in my mind but in my heart, that the Lord would walk with me every step of the way. I was asking for help and the Lord was answering me.

The message was the one Jesus had given to His apostles: *Follow Me.* Not quick, not easy, but simple and straightforward.

After hearing the message, I knew that I had to follow Him and part of that would mean forgiving my mother and the boys who had violated me. Anger had been eating at me like a cancer, but I felt the remedy go all through my body when I stood up and accepted the invitation to Christ.

Later, I made myself rise above the pain of the past and did something nearly unbelievable. I called my aging mom.

I forgave my mother.

I then forgave myself for harboring self-hate.

The past was just that – a time gone, never to be repeated. What mattered now was now and later.

When I decided not to let the past control me, other feelings began to awaken in me. I prayed intensely and asked God to forgive the three boys. I forgave them as I had forgiven my mother, and myself.

I asked God to restore me to my original state, to who He had in mind when He created me which way before me being violated.

Within months, my desire turned toward women. I have been happily married for 18 years. I have three children, prayer, and hope.

By reaching out to the Lord, through the pain and sorrow, I discovered a loving God awaiting me, healing me. I found that life is not just shame and anger – it is also a time of new direction, new life. It is never too late to pray and ask God to line us up with His Divine Design. We are all God's creations.

WHEN THE OUTSIDE COMES IN

***

Prayer: Dear Lord, look upon us with compassion. We struggle with the harsh circumstances of life but long for forgiveness and hope. We find hope each day, in the Bible, in your Holy Word, in constant prayer. When we focus on You, our lives here on earth change. We transform. We heal. We see that You are offering us passage to greater glory in heaven. Help us to know that only you can complete the work you began in us. And only you can restore our virtue and purpose.

May we transform our lives and the lives of everyone around us with your Holy Word.

Thank you for this life, thank You for the life to come in Your heavenly presence. Amen.

The Truth Shall Set You Free

Competition, jealousy, rivalry...what propels a person to act the way he does? Even the most dazzling life is finite – it will come to an end. Then what? Has that person prepared for what is to come?

The following story presents a compelling mix of thoughts, feelings and actions. Picture yourself in the role of the main character, his friend and the person from Human Resources. How would you act in each circumstance?

In the heat of the moment, a proper course of behavior may be hard to find. The Bible offers clear guidelines for behavior: "Do not think of yourself more highly than you ought, but rather think of yourself with sober judgment, in accordance with the measure of faith God has given you" (Romans 12:3).

Again, the Bible shows the way for decent

WHEN THE OUTSIDE COMES IN

behavior:

"Do not repay anyone evil for evil. Be careful to do what is right in the eyes of everybody. If it is possible, as far as it depends on you, live at peace with everyone (Romans 12:17)."

***

I had made it. I was enjoying a great job. The pay was incredible. I was lucky to have such a job in a time when so many people were losing theirs due to layoffs, cutbacks, economic hard times.

The corporate world is tough and competitive. I felt a man needed all the advantages he could get to move ahead. Sometimes this meant doing unethical tactics as I had done to place me ahead of the competition. I became so delusional and full of myself that I had the nerve to tell someone what I had done.

Yes, out of sheer ignorance, I confided in a friend of mine that I had faked having a Masters Degree on my resume. Having it on my resume helped me get my very high-paying job. *The experience I had in life was certainly the equivalent of a Master's. I had "earned" a Master's in Business, in a way. So why not put it on a resume?* That's what I reasoned.

About six years later, I was still working at the company. My friend started working there also. Fast forward four more years. I'd risen to a senior position.

My so-called friend, who now had been there four years, had been considered for the same position. He had gained the same amount of experience I had while he was working for another company.

In the end, I was promoted and he was not. I didn't know jealousy was brewing. We were old buddies, right?

Just as I settled into my new position, Human Resources called me into the office with documented proof of my fake Master's Degree.

Unless I could prove differently, I had to be demoted or resign. The demotion would put me in the same office with the snitch. I had too much pride and anger at that point, so I resigned.

As I was cleaning out my desk, the friend walked by and said, "I see you're cleaning out my new office." He confirmed my suspicion. He was the one who had told Human Resources about my Master's Degree claim on my resume. He had done it to shove me out of my job and take my place. I was livid. I wanted to kill him.

I was bitter for years and wished all kinds of evil on him. I started developing headaches and backaches that I attributed to getting old. I was 32 at the time.

I read something about some pains being associated with a failure to forgive. This caught my attention. I thought of when the pains first started and realized it was right after the event with Human Resources and the loss of my job.

I could continue to be bitter, resentful, filled with hate, but the only thing that would do is give me more aches and pains. Continued pain could lead to something worse. I was in a downward spiral. I needed to do something drastic.

It took almost everything I had, but I made a conscious effort to start the forgiveness process that someone had recommended to me. I had to concentrate on the friend I now despised, relive the humiliation, then rise from the bottom of it all and bring myself to forgive him.

This was business of a different type. It wasn't "Business As Usual," hating my former friend as I usually did. It wasn't competing for a better job in the business world. This was the business of the soul. This was what people prayed about. This was what people turned to the Bible for, to find the words of forgiveness and follow them. It was all there, laid out in black and white.

It took two long months of concentrated effort, but one day I woke up feeling great and no longer had ill feelings about the old friend. I had forgiven him as best I could, releasing him from the bitterness in my heart.

When I did, I also released the headaches and backaches from my body. The physical pains were completely related to the emotions pains I had lived with for years.

Things aren't perfect now. They aren't the way they were between my friend and me in the early days. I really do wish him well, though. However, I must say that I don't choose to completely reconcile with him because I know his trustworthiness has its limitations.

I also realize that I had to seek my own forgiveness for what I had said and done at that company. When I said I had a Master's Degree on my resume, I was misrepresenting myself, and it was a lie. In the Kingdom of God, there is no room for false representation. We have to be true, no matter

WHEN THE OUTSIDE COMES IN

what.

***

Prayer: Dear Heavenly Father, You inspired your apostle, Paul, so that he could communicate Your Word to a fallen world. Paul wrote timeless letters about personal responsibility, forgiveness and love. He wrote to the Romans, "The hour has come for you to wake up from your slumber, because our salvation is nearer now than when we first believed" (Romans 13:12).

Awaken us from our slumber, Lord; help us rise from jealousies, deceits and anger to stand in Your heavenly light. Let us put on the armor of light that protects us from darkness. This we ask in Your Name. Amen.

Not Very Neighborly

The Bible offers God's Holy Word to us. These priceless words teach us love, comfort, understanding and direction. Reading the Bible on a regular basis will provide answers to many questions in life. It will restore broken hearts. It will lift us from dull indifference to greater purpose.

In the following story, a young man finds himself on a wrong path. He begins to see that certain directions in life only lead to dead ends. Read along as he makes dramatic choices that change his life.

***

When I was 15, my parents asked the next door neighbor, Ms. Paulette, to check in on me while they went to a funeral out of town. Ms. Paulette was 43. She was like a mom to everyone -- I thought.

The second day my parents were gone, she came over and just walked into the house without knocking. I had on a T-shirt and underwear. She started talking about my body and how much I resembled my 'fine-looking' daddy. The next thing I knew we were having sex. I never told my parents, but Ms. Paulette must have told some of the other single women. All of them started asking me to cut their grass or help paint the house for a few dollars, but I got *a lot more than money from them.*

By the time I was 19, I was tired of females and downright hated them, which is why I took advantage of them just as they had done to me. I broke their hearts every chance I could. Then I met a woman who had been spending a lot of time with God so I couldn't play the normal games on her. She intrigued me. She told me about myself as if she had a microscope to my heart.

We started studying the Bible together. In all honesty, I started out doing it to impress this woman hoping I could then make her another notch under my belt. I even read the Bible two and three days before our scheduled study time so I could throw scripture at her to further gain her trust.

Then the next thing I knew, I was hooked. Not on the woman but on reading the Bible. I found a connection to the Holy Word that I had not thought possible. They weren't just words on a page. I almost felt as if the Lord was speaking directly to me, getting through my thoughts and reaching my soul in new ways.

I had not known this was possible. I wouldn't have believed it. Somehow, though, I was ready to change. I began searching for something outside of the same old routines. I wasn't just tired of the same old ways in life. I was ready for something new.

The rest is history. I finally understood how I needed to get healthy. It could only start with forgiveness. If God could forgive, then I needed to learn how to do so, too.

Most of the women who tainted my childhood and my idea about women are no longer on this earth, so I can't tell them they are forgiven. But I have verbally named them one by one along with what they did to me and said "I forgive you and I'm setting myself free."

And I took a step that head me extremely nervous. I called all of the women (those I could locate) I had mistreated and asked for their forgiveness. I was met with mixed emotions- some laughed, some cried, some forgave,

WHEN THE OUTSIDE COMES IN

some hung up, and others cussed me out with words I can't repeat.

I started there, and here I am pushing forward to have healthy relationships with women. Most of all, I am trying to keep a healthy relationship with the Lord. Somehow, I know the rest will fall into place as it should.

***

With God, all things are possible. No one is beneath His notice. We are all His creatures. The Psalms were written as songs of sorrow, penitence, thanksgiving and joy. Psalm 51 beautifully prays for forgiveness: "Have mercy on me, O God, according to your unfailing love; according to Your great compassion blot out my transgressions." The Psalm continues with a plea for God's mercy and a cleaning and purification.

Whether we forgive someone or seek forgiveness for ourselves, we are experiencing true cleansing and purification. Our soul starts anew.

PRAYER: Dear Lord, sometimes in life we feel desperate and alone. We feel used, defeated. We feel anger.

We turn to you, Lord, as a light through our darkest hours. Through Your Holy Word, we begin to see ourselves not as victims but as victors who walk in Your path.

When He walked upon the earth, Jesus had the world against Him. They crucified Him so that h]He might die for our sins. Let us renew our lives and the lives of those around us. Help us follow Your Word each and every day. Amen.

The Minister, My Wife, And Me
(M. Richards)

David was a man after God's own heart yet, he fell short when he sinned against God by committing fornication with another man's wife (Bathsheba) (2 Sam. 11, 12). It didn't stop there, he also impregnated her then had her husband positioned in the battlefield where he could be killed (2 Sam 11:14-24). David thought this would cover his tracks, but God sees all.

David paid for his sins and eventually had a repenting heart. God forgave David and restored his virtue. Although many still see David as an exemplary man who had weaknesses and was subject to failure, we should ultimately look to the infallible One as our example, Jesus Christ.

***

My wife was a member of her church for five years. I was raised Muslim and wasn't that interested in going to a

Christian church, so my wife usually attended church alone.

I was not a practicing Muslim. I ate a few ribs sometimes and drifted away from a lot of the customs over the course of many years. However, once I reached the age of 27, my interest actually shifted toward Christianity- but I never told a soul.

So, at 33 I found myself with a wife who spent what seemed like night and day in church. And she really didn't help the situation when she'd come home telling me what her pastor said about our marriage and me with some scripture about us being "unequally yoked". It almost sounded as if he was trying to get her to divorce me.

For years, my wife prayed, sang songs, anointed my pillow, and fussed to get me to go to church. I didn't go but I did start watching Christian television and even watched her pastor a few times.

Each time I watched my wife's church service, I couldn't help but wonder how she had gotten so caught up in a mega-ministry because she hated crowds. And how was she getting up close and personal with a pastor who had over 5,000 people in attendance. Certainly, he had more pressing issues than our marriage.

WHEN THE OUTSIDE COMES IN

Then the church's anniversary celebration rolled around again for the 5th time since we had gotten married. There was supposed to be a special program on Sunday in honor of this accomplishment and my wife tried everything to get me to go. I wouldn't budge. However, I did plan to watch it on t.v.- but that was my little secret.

When she stormed out of the house and sped off in the car, I felt a little uneasy about not going. It was strange feeling that way considering this was not my first time sending her to church alone- she always went alone. I tried everything I could to shake that feeling but nothing worked. Almost 40 minutes later, I found myself driving up to the church and searching for a parking space. I couldn't believe it.

I'd finally zig-zagged through the huge parking lot, parked in a space and walked for what seemed like a mile before finally entering the church. I was so tired I almost went back to my car, but I was a little out of breath and needed to sit down. The doors to the sanctuary were open and the pew in the back offered me just what I needed- a seat.

After I pulled myself together, I stood up and

scanned the crowd for my wife. There were so many people in there that searching each pew made my eyes hurt and the people were talking entirely too much. My head started throbbing. I knew then exactly why I preferred television over being there.

Before I knew it, the service started and it took me on a serious ride. Between the loud music, people seemingly out of control in the isles, my aching head, then finally a 20 minute sermon that I could have enjoyed if not for the boisterous folks around me, I felt like a person who had gone asleep in his own home but woke up in a different country- confused.

When it was all over, I stood around in the back and hoped to find my wife before she left out. As the people ever so slowly weaved their way through the isles and finally out of the doors I became exhausted by just watching and plopped down on another pew. I scanned the thinning crowd some more and finally spotted my wife. But she wasn't walking toward the exits, she was headed toward the pulpit where the pastor was greeting, consoling, counseling, etc.

I watched my wife stand at the end of the line

WHEN THE OUTSIDE COMES IN

patiently for what seemed like forever. I thought about walking up there but opted to save my energy for that long walk through the parking lot to my car. Not to mention that I wasn't in the mood for being double teamed by her and the pastor about my lack of church attendance. So I waited a little longer.

The sanctuary was almost empty when my wife reached the front of the line. After shaking hands with the pastor and having a brief conversation, they both walked away and exited out another doorway together. I asked one of the few parishioners left where those mystery doors lead to and was told "they lead to the administrative offices".

I waited a few more minutes then decided to face the music. I made the dreaded stroll from the back of the huge church to the front then out of the doors and down a long hallway.

When I finally reached the door with the pastor's name on it, I reached to knock but heard laughter, so I stood there listening for a minute. *More laughter. Then silence.* Almost by instinct I opened the door. And there they were in an embrace and kissing as if trying to find the answer to life's most mysterious questions.

I immediately felt an inferno inside of my entire body burning away my foundation, faith, and family. The heat of the fire consuming my life as I knew it sent me rushing into the office and blindly attacking the pastor until I was roughly thrown out of the church onto the cold pavement by two unknown men. I have no idea when or how they got there.

I was never really a praying man but that incident took me past my knees on down to my belly begging, pleading, asking "why?"

My wife immediately moved to her sister's house and it would take weeks for us to finally have a conversation. It turns out that she had been crying on the pastor's shoulder about our marriage and a few consoling hugs, over time, turned into more intimate hugs then finally a kiss. A kiss that I inconveniently interrupted.

I never thought we could move beyond this incident, but each day the weight of the incident became lighter. It would take 18 months before my wife and I fully reconciled. Then it would take another six months after that before we, together, found another church to attend.

My wife's ex-pastor has long since apologized to

us, but even if he hadn't I would have still forgiven him as I forgave my wife.

I must admit that Allah didn't help me through this one. I went straight to the real God who has a Son named Jesus. After I was baptized and filled with the Holy Spirit at our new church, I knew I had to release all that has ever pained me in order for the Lord to hear and grant my prayers.

After I chose to forgive them, not only did a cloud lift off my life but an ulcer in my stomach healed. I also realized that when people are often in the midst of doing wrong they really don't count up all of the costs or think in detail about how their actions can adversely affect everyone and everything around them.

So when I was praying to God one of the many things I said was, "I forgive them because they knew not the extent of what they were doing."

This was the worst thing I had ever experienced in life but some how God gave me the strength to endure and through this I've learned to depend on Him for everything else. So when the issues of life get too heavy all I know how to do now is –let go and let God.

PRAYER: My Heavenly Father, you are the one true and all powerful God. Thank you for giving us the perfect example of forgiveness and perfection. Help us to look upon no man as infallible. Your Word actually says "In the last days the very elect may be deceived" (Matt 24:24). So when we are let down by those we've chosen to trust, let us turn to you knowing that you will never leave or forsake us.

Help us never to use the example of one person as a label for everyone else. Thank you Lord for giving us new mercy every morning, along with the miracle of change and the dulling of pain everyday. You are so awesome. Hallelujah! It is in Your Mighty Name I Pray, Amen.

3

FROM BEHIND PRISON WALLS

To forgive is to set a prisoner free and discover that the prisoner was you.
Lewis B. Smedes

FROM BEHIND PRISON WALLS

ADOPTED TWICE
aka
FORGIVEN FOR THE PAST
(The Briant George Story)

I'm an adopted child in two ways. First - because I was a child born out of wedlock, and my mother was given the ultimatum to either put me up for adoption or face a bitter divorce (along with the possibility of losing all her kids in a custody battle), it seemed best that I be put up for adoption. My grandmother, with the help of her attorney, fought for the right to be made my legal guardian and won.

I have many fond memories growing up. Surrounding me were aunts, uncles and cousins who showered me with attention at family functions and around the house. I didn't have a lot of material possessions other kids my age had, but our house was filled with love and laughter. (Money doesn't buy that, does it?).

My grandmother loved God intensely, and she raised me in a healthy Christian environment. I was instructed in the things of God and the ways of the Bible. We attended church frequently. I was a good student in school; well liked, respected, and happy.

A highlight of my growing up was the first time I met my mother, her husband and my five brothers and sisters at their home in Fayetteville, N.C. I also recall feeling incredulous that my family had a house big enough to have multiple bedrooms; 3 bathrooms; a den; a nice-sized kitchen, and a swimming pool in their back yard.

This was so different from my meager surroundings back home. The entire trip left an inerasable mark upon my young mind, and gave me a deep heart-felt longing to be united with my family – wondering why I was living apart from them and in the neighborhood I was in.

Before going to Fayetteville for the visit, I hadn't really thought much about the surroundings I was in. But shortly thereafter, it evidently did begin to matter, because rebellion began to manifest in me. Self-pity was the "gas" that fueled my engine.

I started associating myself with all the *underprivileged* people, for all the wrong reasons. I began to smoke, drink alcohol, steal candy and snack items, and other forms of mischief.

Though I didn't realize why I was doing all those things at the time, I look back on it now and realize it was my way of wanting to be accepted and to have "power" over those who had what I couldn't afford to have.

Soon I began stealing bigger things as well as smoking dope. I began to skip school and be late for classes more often than not. At first the chastisement for my rebellion was fearful, until I built up a tolerance for it. My heart hardened, and eventually I quit caring.

It was during that time that I was sexually abused twice by another male. It left me confused – mixed up about my sexuality. For many years after I believed the devil's lie that a man could give to another man what God only intended a woman to share with a man: true "Eros" love!

I then joined a well-known gang in my area and became more "wise" in the ways of evil. I even went so far as to steal from my own family.

I was incarcerated at the age of 16 ... after subjecting my grandmother to countless court appearances. I served 24 months before re-entering society, only to violate parole within 90 days of my release. They sent me back to incarceration.

While incarcerated, my heart grew even more bitter. I served the remainder of my three-year sentence and was released again. Once home, I picked up right where I had left off from before, only by that time I was a little more careful in trying to not get caught again.

All this time my grandmother and other Christians would try to share with me the ways of the Lord, and encourage me to quit running from Him and relinquish authority of my life over to Christ. It went in one ear and out the other unfortunately. I was hell-bent on doing my own thing. I was angry, bitter, and resentful inside, and cared very little how God felt about things.

The way I saw it, He hadn't cared for me at a young age, so why should I care about what He wanted now that I was older?

I look at young men coming into the prison and I can read their life story without ever hearing the details. They are grown up boys just like I was … angry at life for one reason or another (usually a bad home life), bitter in their hearts, harboring resentment … and wanting to get "even" somehow – some way.

Anyone with authority over them threatens to stand in their way of finding a little happiness, and when given the opportunity ... that authority either must be destroyed, or at the least, disobeyed. Most believe authority cannot be trusted ... so the only authority that they will obey is their own, unless it is conveniently self-serving to do otherwise.

I realize there are more men and women on the outside of prison who are just as angry at life (and God) as those who come to prison. When I look at these emotionally scarred people, I want to share with them that submitting to the authority of Jesus Christ is the most liberating thing a person can do ... but the devil screams through every fiber of their being: "It's the weakest (and scariest) thing a real man could do!" What a lie.

I believe I understand why a lot of people link up with the radical, militant element of the Islamic religion. People with pent up anger, bitterness and resentment in their hearts don't want to change. They want a way to express that anger, and being a "militant for God" is a lot more appealing to some than letting God take away all that pent up anger, bitterness and resentment and replacing it with tolerance, forgiveness, and kindness … which is what the Holy Spirit excels in, wanting to impart to disciples of Jesus Christ, if they will only allow Him to do that.

Anyway … back to the details of how life continued to spiral downward for me. After two years of being on the outside, I was handcuffed again. This time I was sentenced 4 ½ – 9 years, of which I had served 5 ½ years of being on parole.

Once released from prison, I was no different. Sure, part of me wanted change in my life for the better, but I didn't possess the "power" to change – not Christ's power anyway, which is the only power that will heal a hardened and embittered heart like I had.

I then was stabbed by over half a dozen guys, but fortunately, my wounds were superficial compared to what they could have been. I now realize God's hand of mercy and loving-kindness had protected me, though I didn't realize it at the time. I was blinded by the "god of this world": Satan (see 2 Corinthians 4:4 for understanding) – because I refused to serve the Lord Jesus Christ.

By that time I had amassed a daily cocaine habit of 4-6 grams, and at first I was able to buy these drugs without much problem. As time passed, my financial resources began to dry up as my dependence for more cocaine increased, which almost always becomes the case for cocaine users.

This forced me to take more drastic measures to come up with money to support my addiction, and it led me to stealing from anybody and everybody, no matter how close I was to them.

A major robbery spree lasted a little over two months – sparking a citywide manhunt for my arrest by New York City authorities. I eluded them for about six weeks.

While running from the law, constantly running and looking over my shoulder -- God was still reaching out to me – pleading with me to quit running from Him and surrender to His authority and lordship. While holed up at one of my hideouts – high on drugs and out of my mind – my grandmother and two of my aunts came to where I was [To this day I still don't know how they knew where I was hiding, though God obviously showed them somehow.

They laid hands on me, anointed me with oil, and prayed God's protection, provision, and subsequent salvation for me. Then they pleaded with me to surrender to the authorities out of fear that I might possibly be fatally wounded in a gun battle or any number of other things that could harm me.

It has been said that God often reaches out and delivers man at his lowest point … just when he hits rock bottom. (Actually, God is reaching out all the time, but it takes us hitting rock bottom before we're willing to seriously begin walking in proper relationship with Him). My "rock bottom" was quickly approaching. I began to think about my past life.

What did I have to show for it? In and out of prison most of my life; always in trouble with the law; disgrace and dishonor to my family. Lying, stealing, robbing, involvement in homosexuality; just to name a few of the things my life was about.

I decided the best way out was to take my life. Not with a gun, mind you, or by drug overdose, but by suicide nonetheless, albeit in a very convoluted way. I chose to have sex with two known, obvious A.I.D.S. carriers. Somehow I rationalized it was my way of getting it over with without all the mess.

FROM BEHIND PRISON WALLS

When I was arrested, I was close to 30 pounds under weight. I was dirty, smelly and tired. I knew the constant tiredness in my body was due to the AIDS virus taking its toll. I was weak physically. I thought to myself: Good. I can quietly die in prison and no one will even notice.

Unbeknown to me … God had a different kind of death in mind for me. It's the same "death" most have to go through before they truly become saved, born again teachable disciples of Jesus Christ. It's called: "Dying to selfish desires." (Followed with coming alive in Christ Jesus! He has to kill our "old selfish, sinful nature" to impart His "new God nature" in us. Read the sixth chapter of Romans for some understanding of this).

For the first time in almost 20 years I picked up a Bible and began to read it. I even began to pray occasionally, even though my motives weren't always right or pure. I know God answered some of those prayers, so the spiritual seed was planted and was slowly being watered for me to be truly spiritually born again.

I was offered 20-50 years at first (which I promptly refused) then it changed to 25 years to life. Finally I was offered a cop-out (plea) of 15 years to life. This too I refused. However, I began to witness some strange things occurring both around me and within me: an attitude change.

Strangely, I began to run into Christians almost everywhere. At the prison I was housed in; at court; some Correction Officers: there were Christian believers all around me, and they showed me the love of Jesus Christ continuously. They told me they were praying for me, and they took the time to answer questions I had about the Bible and God. It was unreal how so many Christians were placed in my path during that time: it could only have been God orchestrating it!

One of my attorney's advice was to take the cop-out plea and run, because according to him, I was doomed. I told him, "If it's God's will, I'll either be released, or found guilty. I'm trusting Him to determine what happens to me." His response was, "It's a little too late to become religiously inclined now, Mr. George!" (He didn't realize God's mercy and grace are never too late).

One day I was in the cellblock -- totally bored with nothing to do. I came up with this silly notion to take a small Gideon's New Testament Bible and get near my cell gate and perform a "mock sermon." Don't ask me why I came up with this ridiculous idea at the time. I began reading from several passages in the Gospels, and then I related how selfish it was for the guys not to share their cigarettes and drugs, but in a playful and chiding manner.

The guys joined in and began to shout mocking "Amen's!" and "Hallelujahs!" ... encouraging me to keep on "preaching." Everyone joined in with the mockery and it brought excitement to replace our boredom.

Then a very strange thing happened. The Holy Spirit took charge without my realizing it. In fact, I have no recollection of all that I even said, but there was no doubt the presence of God was on me. The "mocking sermon" suddenly changed to a "**real** sermon!"

Officers and inmates alike began to comment: "If you got serious, you could be a really good preacher! Can you imagine **this**: sinners encouraging another sinner to preach God's Word? It was a very strange "experience" to say the least! I was stunned by it.

Not long after I was pronounced guilty of 16 counts of robbery one, four counts of burglary, possession of a loaded firearm, and possession of a controlled substance, I was sentenced under the Persistent Felony Offender Statute.

Naturally at first I felt devastated. I became despondent … then furious. I then vowed to be the most violent, rebellious, troublesome inmate there was! As I made my third trip to Upstate (prison) I saw my whole life flash before me, which caused a deep feeling of remorse and regrets as I thought many places I was passing by would be the last time I would ever see them in this life.

I assumed I would never see my family members again. I had no children so certainly I would never have children come to visit me. All of these thoughts, and many more crossed my mind – needless to say, not being pleasant.

Upon arrival at "Reception," in prison, I was made to wait until last to process in. Rather than simply get processed in like everyone else, I was called into the Supervisor's Office to talk with the Sergeant, Lieutenant, and Captain to be screened. Because of my case (involving a politician), an attempted escape, and the extensive amount of time I was given (and my high-profile status), I was placed on the security watch-list.

    When I entered my room I was told to sit down, upon which I was promptly informed that the prison authorities were aware of my prior attempted escape, and to not try to repeat my actions, because they would be futile. I was then asked how I felt about the sentence I had received and that they realized I had a large amount of time, and did I feel myself to be a possible threat to others, or myself? I paused for a considerable amount of time and responded facetiously, "I don't know. I might kill myself, or kill someone else. It all depends on how I'm feeling at the moment."

    I was told to step back outside for awhile and I would be notified shortly of where I would be housed. Little did I know God was behind the scenes orchestrating the events. Shortly afterwards I was escorted to the Mental Health area of the hospital to see a psychiatrist, where the same questions asked me previously were basically repeated over again. I told the Doc the same thing.

    I was then recommended for - and subsequently sent to - a "strip cell" where a person is not given any sheets, shoelaces, clothes and other items one might use to kill themselves with. I was put under a 24-hour suicide watch, but praise God, I was allowed a Bible.

After pressing and pleading with the medical staff about going to a regular cellblock, and receiving my clothes and some bed sheets, I was finally scheduled to see the doctor to be considered for possible release from "suicide watch."

I entered the doctor's office to be greeted by a pleasant looking Chinese-American doctor, who seemed abnormally soft spoken and polite. He asked me a number of questions, all to which I answered honestly. After some time he leaned back in his chair with a thoughtful look on his face and said, "Mr. George, you don't seem crazy to me. Rather you seem to be highly intelligent, well-mannered, and articulate. You don't appear to be anything like the guy described here in this folder."

I mumbled some response and just shrugged my shoulders, not really knowing how to respond to that. Next he asked me what happened to bring all of this about? I answered, "I really don't know. I guess a lot of mistakes and bad choices."

Then he asked a rather odd question. "Mr. George,

FROM BEHIND PRISON WALLS 99

do you have your ticket?"

I informed him that I had yet to be written a "misbehavior report" since my arrival at Upstate.

He responded, "No, Mr. George. I mean ... do you have your ticket to heaven?"

I answered, "I don't know; I hope so."

He said I need to be sure, and proceeded to share the gospel with me. (The "gospel" is the message that the second person of the Godhead died for the sins of humanity – that being Jesus Christ, or The Word [see the first chapter of John] - and was I willing to trust God the Father that His wrath was instantly removed from me if I turned my life over to Jesus Christ?]. After that he told me about the services held there on Sundays, and how good the ministers were, and encouraged me to go and check them out. He took me off the 24-hour watch and placed me on regular status.

That following Sunday I was led by the Holy Spirit to the Protestant Service, though I didn't understand it all at the time. The way the officers were directing people to sit, I should have ended up in the back of the chapel. Instead, I was not only in the front pew, but also directly in front of the podium. Oh my ... was God ever answering the prayers of my grandmother and her friends!

I don't remember the message; the text; the name of the preacher: nothing. All I know is that God was speaking directly to me that Sunday morning, and the conviction of the Holy Spirit was heavily upon me, as God's anointed word went forth. When the sermon ended and the preacher gave an invitation for prayer at the front, I quickly scrambled out of my seat and moved to the pulpit.

Before over 200 hardened criminals I confessed my sins, and asked Jesus Christ into my heart as I wept like a baby. What a beautiful encounter with God it was!

When I got back to my cell ... I was still crying rivers of tears, but something was different inside; something very much different. I felt clean and I sensed lightness, as if all the burdens I was carrying around for so long had finally been lifted off. As I gazed out of my window toward the highway through the pouring rain ... crying tears of rejoicing and thanksgiving ... I felt like the Holy Spirit was impressing upon me that just like the rain was washing away the filth and dirt from off of the streets outside, so were my sins being washed away in like manner. I just stood for a good while and worshipped God.

After that I read my Bible for a while, allowing the Holy Spirit to feed me and comfort me through it. Thus I was spiritually born again that day, as Jesus speaks of in John 3:3.

I am proud and thankful to say God has completely transformed me according to 2 Corinthians 5:17, and I am a brand new creation: Therefore, if anyone is in Christ, he is a new creation; old things have passed away; behold, all things have become new.

I don't' smoke, curse, drink, get high, fornicate, gamble, practice lying, read filthy books, cheat, talk down on people, nor have I had a fight with anyone for almost 10 years…by the grace of God! I love preaching and teaching and witnessing about the goodness of God every chance I get. God has allowed me to minister in song and I write poetry and other articles about spiritual things as I feel impressed of the Holy Spirit to do so.

My sentence has since been modified to 50 years to life (from 400 years) and I am confident that God will open the doors for me to leave prison when the time is right. God has blessed me super-abundantly in the past eight years as I have grown in my walk with the Lord, and understanding of His holy Word. He has kept me, protected me, guided and directed me – and He has demonstrated His faithfulness to me more times than I can remember. God has even blessed me with a wonderful friend, wife, and Christian woman to be my helpmate. He sent her here all the way from San Francisco, California … 3,500 miles away!

I just want to say in closing that God loves **you**, whoever you are reading this, and He can deliver your from any sin or stronghold imaginable; He can take your hurt and pain away you have known much of your life, if you'll allow Him. If His love reached down to the pit of hell for me – one so undeserving – He'll surely reach down for **you**. He's just a prayer away … no matter how hopeless you feel life is.

I started my testimony by saying I was adopted two ways. You read about my first. The second is my "spiritual" adoption. I have been adopted into the family of God. As scripture assures all born again believers in Jesus Christ, it reads: For you did not receive the spirit of bondage again to fear, but you received the Spirit of

adoption by whom we cry out, "Abba, Father." The Spirit Himself bears witness with our spirit that we are children of God, and if children, then heirs – heirs of God and joint heirs with Christ, if indeed we suffer with Him, that we may also be glorified together-- (Romans 8:15-17).

I'm quite certain the suffering I have experienced that put me in prison was caused mostly by anger and rebellion and selfishness, and of course, ultimately my drug addiction. But no matter what wrong and unwise choices I made in the past, the future is what now matters. I've been forgiven for the past, and the future lasts for eternity.

If God grants me the opportunity to preach to sinners filled with anger and resentment and bitterness like used to have, then to Him be all the glory! (I guarantee that if I get the chance, it surely won't be any "mock" preaching either!). The many years I have to spend in prison serving out my sentence is like a blink of an eye compared to eternity.

Sure ... it's no picnic in prison, but now I have someone who sits in my cell with me day and night, and never leaves me nor forsakes me. It's the Spirit of Jesus Christ. He's both inside me, and yet He fills the entire universe with His love! He is what I live for.

I DON'T HATE GOD ANYMORE
(*The John Miller Story*)

Just before my youngest sister, Seri was born, a terrible tragedy struck my family. Our kin was stealing whiskey from our father's stock. From what I understand, there were several family members killing each other. All I can remember is hiding in my bedroom while all the shooting was going on outside. Then I heard someone coming through the back door next to my bedroom. When I looked out, I saw my brother, James, coming down the hall. My sister Ruby, shot and killed him and my next oldest brother Sammie, shot my sister Ruby, badly wounding her. Our family was broken up then.

Born the first day of April, 1949. I was born in Clarksdale, Mississippi, to John Henry and Sarah Almedy Miller. I had four older brothers, one older sister, and five younger sisters. All my brothers and. sisters were born about one year apart.

My mother, who was a good woman and a God-fearing person, always tried to do the right thing with regards to all others, and she always took good care of all her children.

I do not remember my father too much, just what I was told about him. I was told that he was a drunk whiskey-making bootlegger, and a horrible person. He worked as an Operator and a Woodsman, Lumberjack.

After the tragic shooting incident in my family... those that weren't killed or carried to jail... left the state. My mother moved from Mississippi to Arkansas with my five younger sisters, my brother (who was one year older than me), and myself. We relocated in a little town in Arkansas. We lived on a farm that raised cotton, soybeans, corn, and hay.

The next couple of years were not a pleasant time. My mother was left with seven small kids, no money, no husband, and no relatives to help. She was too old to work the farm steadily. Things were getting worse by the day, but there was always alot of love and kindness for our family.

We would walk three or four miles to a little church to pray and thank God. I can remember my mother praying to God and thanking him for all our circumstances. She prayed for other people's sicknesses and any other problems that they were having in their lives. I confess that I did not understand why we thanked God for us being poor. All I could think about was how I felt, and all of my wants.

After awhile, my mother had no choice, but to take me and my brother out of school to work in the fields with her. We had to work for other farmers, and we lost everything we had. My brother and I were too small to work alone so we worked together as one.

We both worked ten hours a day for $2.50. My mother, brother, and I worked thirty hours a day, combined time, for $5.00.

Times were very hard, for a woman with seven children in the late 1950s and 1960s.

We were not the only family that was poor. There were other families with sick and elderly people. Thank God that my family was in good health. I hadn't thought much about our way of life until after a few years.

I then began to notice that some people were driving new, shiny cars, and lived in nice big houses with family living in other states coming to visit them. I wondered if I had family living in other states, and if so, why didn't they come to visit *us*? Where was my daddy?

Why didn't he come home? I asked my mother about my father, and if we had any other family. That is when I found out my daddy was a drunkard, and he had been one for a number of years. His family wouldn't have anything to do with him or us.

My mother did have one sister, Aunt May. I went to visit her once. She was a widow woman, with a mean attitude toward me. I thought to myself that same day that if I was ever married and had kids, they would never have to live like me. I rejected everybody, and hated everybody, including myself.

For the next couple of years, I drank alcohol and frequently assaulted people. I blamed everybody else for my problems. I had no friends, and didn't want any. I was told that I was just like my daddy. Part of me didn't like the way I was living my life, but I accepted being mean to others because it was the one thing I *was* good at.

I got married in 1964 to Mary Steward from Oklahoma. She was part Native American (Indian), and part Spanish. We had five boys and one girl together. I worked for Ford Motor Company and made good money. I was quite happy with my family. I quit drinking, and stayed out of trouble for about 25 years. My wife worked as a teenage counselor, and she was a good mother. Our kids were never much trouble to us.

Our oldest son met a girl, got married, and moved to Holland, MI where they had three children, two girls and a boy. In 1993, my oldest son got sick. By the end of 1993, all five of our sons were sick. By 1994, all five sons died. I didn't know what to do. My life went to hell in less than one year. We lost everything paying hospital bills. I was drinking everyday, and I blamed God for the death of our sons.

When my wife started preaching to me about God, I got mad and ran her and my daughter off. I told them that they could just go live with their God. I told her she was the reason for our kids' deaths. I didn't want anything to do with her or God, and told her to just leave me alone.

I regretted doing that as soon as I said it, but I was to tied up in my own self-pity and anger - not accepting responsibility for my actions nor making wise choices, and not realizing I was taking the bait of Satan. All I wanted to do was drink and use drugs to escape the pain. That is all I did everyday and every night for over a year. Then I started *selling* drugs and stealing cars to finance my alcohol and drug habit. I used up all the money I could borrow or steal from people.

Finally I started getting into trouble with the law - wondering why it took them so long to catch me. I was in and out of jail for my alcohol, drug, and criminal assault. I was out of jail on bond for an assault charge, but I knew that I was going to see prison time before I even went to court. I already made three years probation from a prior conviction of assault. I had given up all hope, and continued to blame God, along with everybody else for my troubles. I continued using alcohol, drugs, and committing criminal assault.

I landed back in prison a short time later. I continued my violent behavior in prison by assaulting other prisoners and staff. When the prison Psychologist came to talk to me, I assaulted *him*. After a year, he came back to talk to me again, and told me that we had something in common. He had lost his daughter. He told me about some of his personal problems and asked if I believed in God.

Then he asked if I would talk to him about some of my problems. After I opened up and talked to him, he told me that he could help me if I would let him. He said that I was living in the past, and needed to accept responsibility for my actions. If I didn't change, I would be in prison for the rest of my life. Or worse yet, I would be killed.

That was my wake up call. That same day, April 28th, 1997, I accepted Jesus Christ as my personal Lord and Savior. I prayed to God asking forgiveness for so many things...especially asking Him forgiveness for my hating Him so much for so long...and thanked him for all that He had done for me for dying for my sins - so I wouldn't be judged for them on the Judgment Day.

I adapted a common saying after that: ***"God grant me the serenity to accept the things I cannot change, the courage to change the things I can, and the wisdom to know the difference."***

I began living one day at a time. I began to accept hardship as a means God uses to conform Christian believers into the likeness of Jesus Christ, strange as that sounds to our natural minds. Enduring hardships without allowing bitterness and anger to rise up in us will reap eternal rewards. To the glory of God...I have not had one ticket or been in trouble here in prison since that day I turned my life over to Jesus. I know it's the Holy Spirit who has given me the ability to change.

By God's help, and for His glory, I will keep working on my behavior for the rest of my life. I am so thankful for the spiritual awakening God brought about in my life. I came to Him out of bitter and angry darkness.

I suppose some would think I had every reason to hate Him, and keep hating Him, but you know what? If I would have continued to hate Him...how would I ever be able to make *peace* with Him? It is a very sad thing to be so angry at God that you fail to realize there can be no peace with Him - holding onto your anger and unforgiveness towards Him.

I was holding onto unforgiveness towards Him at an early age and didn't even realize it. People who do that are only hurting themselves, (and sadly, usually those closest to them), I have come to realize.

I want to thank God for Michigan's Macomb Correctional Facility's R.S.A.T. program (Residential Substance Abuse Treatment), and also the I.O.P program.

These programs offer many opportunities. In attending them, I have learned facts about drug use and

FROM BEHIND PRISON WALLS 113

criminal behavior, why a person acts the way they do, and how to change from using my behavior that may harm me and others, to one that will benefit me and others.

While here in prison, I've also worked diligently to develop skills that will help me enhance social relationships, including how to be a better father, friend, and partner. I also have developed problem solving skills, and realistic personal goals, along with strategies for achieving my goals. I have learned to feel good about myself, and take pride in who I am instead of hating myself...and I owe it all to God who saved me from self-destruction.

FORGIVEN SEX CRIME OFFENDER
(The Robert Swift Story)

I first heard the voice of God ringing in my ear when I was eight years old, and longed to know more about our Savior and Lord. Because I was young and innocent, the devil -knowing my weaknesses -took and snatched me up before I was able to get myself rooted deep in Christ Jesus.

My dad and mom got a divorce when I was nine, and that deceiver led me to believe that it was my fault. I put the blame and shame onto myself, something many young children tragically do in divorce situations. This caused me to fall into a saddened state of perpetual depression.

Before the divorce, I was sexually molested by someone I knew and trusted. I felt this too was my fault, and it sunk me even further into depression and shame. To top that off, my dad used to beat me when I had done something wrong, and he was a drunk. My mom could wale on me just as good as Dad did also.

That didn't bother me at this time though, because I was told that it was for my own good. Because of my love and respect for my folks, I believed them, and trusted that they knew what was best for me. I mean, after all, they were my parents, right?!

I must say that I stayed in that sad and depressed state though the whole time that the devil had his hold on me.

When I turned 14, a friend showed me how to masturbate. This felt good, and it could take away my depression; albeit for a few minutes at the most. Oh, I suppose that I could of used drugs – booze, and probably would of, if I had been introduced to them.

Any one of these things would have helped curb my depressed state for short periods of time, yet could never have taken away my depression completely, something I am aware of now.

So – I turned on to masturbation to ease my suffering, and I would "do it" three, four -sometimes five times a day to feel good, and ease my pain. I figure that I abused my body in this way at least two times a day for thirty years; so you do the math.

The time came when the devil helped me get creative. I got the idea that if this made me feel good, it could make others feel good as well. Because I was depressed, I thought others must be too, so I would help them get 'un-depressed'.

Again, I have to remind readers, I held onto all the hurt that came from the divorce and earlier molestation, thinking I was the cause of it all. After all, I was the key figure that was present at all my calamities. I was completely under a cloud of deception.

Then one day, out of curiosity, I showed a young boy who was feeling blue how to "feel good." He told his mom, who told the police, and I was called in for questioning. In my shame, and wanting to be freed from the devil's stronghold on me – I confessed, but my lawyer was able to get my charges reduced, and I was given probation and counseling.

There I was told that because I was sexually molested, I molested (which is true much of the time in the lives of sex crime offenders). I was confused by this, however, because that meant to me that because my dad was a drunk, I would be a drunk. I hated booze. That way of thinking didn't make sense, and this only caused me to be more mixed up than ever about why I did what I did.

The day came when I thought the only way to be free from my past was to get married, have children, own a nice home, have a good job, and have lots of friends. Yet when I got many of those things, I still carried the burden of my horrible past and eventually went into counseling.

After I obtained worldly counseling void of solid Godly biblical counsel, my curiosity, once again got the better of me, and I touched another boy. When the devil has his spell on you, there is only one way to break that curse. Through the help of God!

That is the reason why my worldly counseling was of no permanent help. When a person is dealing with God and the demonic, only God has permanent and lasting solutions to humanities' problems. Sin is a spiritual issue. God alone holds the wisdom and power to break sin's stranglehold off someone's life.

So - I caught another case, and again I was able to

get the charges reduced: for God was not ready to save, just yet, or perhaps more accurately stated ... I was not ready to surrender to His *Lordship.* To top this all off, I had now developed a fear – a fear of losing everything that I had worked so hard for. So I took the plea to keep from going to prison, which I feared terribly.

It was at this point that I began to really hate myself, and this began to drive me to God for help. Evidently I had not suffered enough yet to be truly and totally sincere with Him however, because the hate would not go away.

In my frustration, I became even more angry at myself. This anger led me to swear like a sailor, and in frustration I began to take out my rage on those around me, something that rage always does if anger is not dealt with. To express itself, rage seeks to destroy: destroy others, or destroy oneself ... or both.

I got two years probation, and more counseling. But nothing had changed, because I still had my loved ones with me to help me feel safe and secure (albeit, it was a false sense of security), thus I was not alone. And what I did not know yet, is that their strength could not defeat the devil.

Then a few years later, I let my out-of-control-curiosity (which I now know to be sexual lust), trap me once more.

I did the unthinkable, yet again. But now I was in complete despair, and cried out to God one more time for help. I believe that it was at this point that God knew that my supplications were sincere and from the heart, because this time I heard that voice. It was the same voice that I had heard when I was eight. And it said, "Just trust in me and everything will be alright."

I caught another case. Three strikes and you're out, right?! But now I hated myself to the point that the fear of losing everything didn't matter anymore. So I decided to put my trust in that voice.

Let me tell you, if I could have committed suicide with the assurance that it would be 100% okay on the other side, I would have. But I couldn't think of a surefire way. So in tears this time, I prayed once again to God, and asked Him for His forgiveness.

I then told my lawyer that I was guilty, and to do whatever he had to do. I was through, and I could no longer go on living this kind of secret, double lifestyle: I wanted my life to end.

My lawyer felt compassion for me, and told me to hang in there for the sake of my children, saying, "They need a father." But what good is a father, I thought, if he cannot control his own sick lust and temper? How is he to teach his children right things, when he is living in the wrong? However, I cannot express what his words did for me. But now it was too late, for I was sentenced to prison for the wrong I had done.

Because I was so emotional when I arrived at prison, they thought that I might be suicidal, so they placed me in a cell next to guards where they could keep an eye on me. Not knowing for sure if God was with me, I began to pray.

I asked God if He was indeed with me. I said, "Show me a sign, Father God. Come in the form of a mouse or something, so I can know for sure that You are here with me."

That night, a mouse ran across my cell room floor. From that very moment, I knew that God was with me. I invited God to come into my heart, and I started to read the

Bible. I knew of God and His Son, Jesus Christ, from my youth, but I never really had a personal relationship with them. Prison changed all that, because now I was all alone. I couldn't run away, and to add to that, no one wanted to have anything to do with me. And why should they? I had betrayed everyone's trust. Nevertheless, this hurt – it hurt real bad. But God knew that this was exactly what I needed.

Someone once said … a root of bitterness is unforgiveness grown up.

What can holding a lifetime of unforgiveness do to people who refuse to forgive their enemies they hate so much? It can get you sent to prison, I can tell you that! It can take you to your grave sooner than you have to die, I can tell you that. It can cause every kind of emotional and physical sickness and disease known to mankind to strike your body. It can cause you loss of confidence in getting a good mate, getting a better job, having a successful marriage, raise normal children, and most important of all … it will remove hindrances in the spirit realm that keeps you at odds with God Himself, and this grieves God dearly, because He wants you to be close to Him. He created you to be close to Him -- intimate with Him.

If you say that you can't forgive someone, God will give you the ability to do it if you will ask Him to, and trust Him to. Please know, forgiving is a decision. It is never a feeling. Feelings of hate and revenge can come and go even after you forgive someone.

God sometimes allows us to be offended as a test. It's a test to see if we'll humble ourselves enough to forgive. God says that if we refuse to forgive others, He'll refuse to forgive us. (Read: Matthew 6:14-15)

To a wise person, forgiveness is never an option. Second only to making Jesus Christ your Savior and Lord … it's the best "spiritual antibiotic" on this planet to prevent terminal disease from taking over one's spirit, soul and body, and ensuring that everything remains healthy between you and your Creator.

I kneeled down in the cell and gave my life to Christ. Even though I lost everything of an earthly nature when I came to prison, as my family abandoned me, and my wife of 17 years divorced me, and all my worldly belongings and friends … I have established a permanent relationship with the living God that remain throughout eternity!

God also took away the swearing, the compulsive masturbating, the sexual lust, the hate, the anger, the malice, the depression, and the shame, and made me a new creature in Jesus Christ: full of love, compassion, long suffering, faith, meekness, joy, peace, gentleness, goodness, and temperance. Praise God!

When he fully opened my eyes, I realized that I had caused a lot of people in my life to have to suffer needlessly. I wept bitterly for this.

BEING ABLE TO FORGIVE THOSE I HATED HAS SET ME FREE
(The Mark Anthony Velez Story)

I was born on July 29, 1963 in Pontiac, Michigan. At the time of my birth my parents were divorced, and both were in their own addictions of alcohol, drugs, sex and all that goes with that lifestyle. I am told that moments after my birth, Child Protective Services threatened to take me away from both of my parents, because they were both in active addiction and not willing to seek help to recover.

I am a product of a bi-racial marriage. I was not wanted by either of my parents, neither did my mother's mother want anything to do with me. As a result of her own prejudice, and because my father's work schedule would not allow him to raise a child … his mother stepped up and chose to raise me.

My Mexican grandma (as I often refer to her) not only wanted to raise me, she wanted to break the generational curse that plagued her family. The curse went back to my grandfather (her husband) and continued on to reach all of her sons.

Growing up, I lived in a very poor area of Pontiac, on Going Street. It was known as the ghetto. In 1969 my father relocated my grandmother and I to a "better" part of Pontiac, and even though we no longer lived in the ghetto, the atmosphere in the home was horrific.

There was a lot of physical, verbal and emotional abuse from my father. Not only did he abuse me, he also abused his own mother. For the most part, my father was an unbearable man.

Despite the chaos, my Mexican grandmother never wavered in her faith. I thank God for the strength he gave her to pray no matter what was going on.

My mother did not have a pivotal role in raising me. When she would come around, she was either drunk or high, and she was physically and verbally abusive. I longed for the acceptance and approval of both my parents, (as every child does), but what I got in return was beatings, being emotionally torn down...ripped apart...shredded... rejected.

Many years of being mistreated chipped away at my heart and hardened my heart with bitterness, low self-esteem, anger, and unrelenting hatred towards *all* people...not just my parents. I can remember hearing, "I hate you!" from my mother, followed by beating after beating.

I remember seeing the rage in my father's eyes as he would hit me, hold a gun to my head, send whores into my room, or chase my Mexican grandmother out of the house because she would confront him about his addiction.

Both my parents used alcohol, heroin and PCP. I would watch as they would shoot up or drink, or both, and would nearly overdose. The hurt that was inside me grew like a cancerous tumor and I became dangerous to myself and others around me.

I became the collateral damage of my parent's addiction, and my Mexican grandmother's worst fear -- the continuation of the generational curse that plagued the men in her family. When I was age ten, my father introduced me to sex by buying me a whore. On the other extreme, at other times he would make me stay away from the house when he had women over by turning on the porch light to let me know he had someone there.

At age 13, I began using alcohol and drugs to cope with the hurt and pain. I also became sexually irresponsible myself, having sex with any girl who was willing to participate. At the same time, I got my girlfriend pregnant many times and made her have abortions.

Life became so painful, I attempted to kill myself one time with a knife to the chest, but the knife broke. I felt that I couldn't even do that right at the time! All my life ... I felt like a failure, and I believed that it was not possible for anyone to love me, or care for me. The repeated rejection from my parents reinforced this belief.

As is sadly so common, as I was abused, I too began to abuse everyone around me. I had no regard for my life or anyone else's. I hated everyone. After all - no one loved me, at least no one that I was aware of.

I was an extremely violent teenager. If I did not get what I wanted, I would take it; I would beat you up for it. If you looked at me wrong - I would beat you up -- looking for any little excuse to vent my frustration, anger and revenge.

My girlfriend and I continued being irresponsible and I became a Dad at 19 and because I did not know how to be a father, I continued to abuse alcohol and drugs, doing the best that I knew how to do to be a Dad.

I would beg and plead to be around my daughter. Her mother would move without telling me where she would be living. I eventually would find them, but because I was always strung out on drugs, my daughter's mother would not allow me to be a part of her life.

The time came when I became like a savage, robbing anyone and everyone that I could in order to be able to buy some drugs. I didn't care who I robbed: drug dealers, other addicts, drug houses, innocent people … it didn't matter, as long as I could get some dope for myself.

With that savage mindset, I began my journey in and out of prison. I was arrested in 1986 for "Breaking and Entering." I was sentenced, through the Michigan Department Of Corrections, to a 2-5 year stay in the MDOC prison system, during which time I went through withdrawals from all the drugs that I had been on, so often wishing that I was dead. I was released on tether after a year of my sentence.

Once I was released, the chaos started again and only got worse. When I had been incarcerated, I had corresponded with a female that I had known in the streets.

She became my girlfriend, and she came to pick me up when I was released on tether. When she came to get me, she came with a large quantity of cocaine. Within one month of my release I was back into my addiction and criminal activities, as if I had never stopped.

Around this same time my daughter and I were temporarily reunited at her baptism. However, my violent behavior destroyed our short-lived reconciliation.

What contributed to that . . . my daughter's godfather -who was like a brother to me had stepped up to the plate and became her father-figure, and shortly after her baptism, her godfather was killed. I vowed to find the person who caused that pain to my little girl (not considering the pain I had *already* caused, or was *going* to cause). Although I felt that I was doing the "honorable thing," I only ended up refueling the anger and hatred that I had lived with from childhood.

I found the person who caused my daughter the pain of losing her godfather, and I tried to kill this person. It didn't matter to me that I was on parole, because I was out of control. I was erupting inside, and did not know how to free myself, yet fortunately I called my parole agent and told him what I had done.

Shortly after calling my parole agent I was arrested and sent back to prison for a short time. During this incarceration my son was born (1988). I was released later that year and married my son's mother. This turned out to be a huge mistake. My new wife and son became "my hostages," as I did not understand the sacredness of matrimony. I continued my terrorism on life through continued drugs and alcohol, and all the sin that came with it.

The years that I have spent in prison were certainly some of the toughest years of my life, yet they pale in comparison to the years I have spent in total spiritual darkness. My worst day in prison with Jesus Christ as my Lord and Savior is ten times better than my seemingly good days in the world without Jesus.

As I have looked back, I can see that God has had His hand on me my whole life. He have me the grace to be able to survive what I had been through. He has given me mercy for my past (both the pain I caused to others, and the pain they gave to me). He has allowed people to love me as He loves us, unconditionally!

Being able to forgive people you hate … no matter what they did to you or how they treated you … is very possible. All it takes is a decision on our part.

Jesus has given me the ability to forgive my parents, and the ability to forgive *myself.* Being able to forgive one's self is one of the most difficult barriers to overcome for many people, as it was me, but with the strength that Jesus Christ provides … it is very much possible!

If you have a nuclear warhead ticking away, about to explode, it has to be disarmed someway. The way to disarm the deadly cancer of hate – bitterness – self-destructive tendencies (which end up trapping people in drugs, alcohol, crime, promiscuous sex, suicide tendencies, abuse to others, desire for revenge, etc.) … is to ***forgive***.

Prayer

To exercise true forgiveness, one must have a real relationship with the One who initiated it. Therefore, if you are not a born again believer/Christian and would like to accept Christ as your Lord and Savior, please repeat this simple prayer.

"Lord, I am a sinner. Please forgive me for all the wrong that I have done. I believe that Jesus is the Son of God and that He died on the cross for me. I confess you as my Lord and Savior, come into my heart and give me the strength to live my life for you. In Jesus' Name, Amen."

**If you have prayed this prayer to accept Jesus Christ into your heart, I welcome you to the family. The next step is to find a Bible-based church so that you can grow in the things of God.

Simple Steps to Forgiveness

Forgiveness is not natural. It is supernatural.

Step 1 – Identify and express your feelings.
Label them as specifically as you can. Think back to what gave rise to these feelings.

- What happened to you?
- Who did this to you?
- When did it occur?

Step 2 – If you have been hurt, you hate.
Some believe it is wrong to hate but, we are supposed to hate what God hates.

- Hate sin, not the sinner. Make sure you distinguish between the two.

Step 3 – Acknowledge your feelings and dismiss the idea of getting even.
Accept your own sense of hurt and vulnerability, then:

- Refuse to be a victim
- Cancel the debt
- Take your life off of 'Pause'
- Allow God to reign supreme in your situation

SIMPLE STEPS TO FORGIVENESS

Your response to evil is not to respond with evil. You've completely forgiven someone when you can pray for God to bless him or her. Just let go and let God.

Step 4 – Forgiveness is both an event and a process.

- Letting an offender off your hooks is an event.
- Finding relief from your own pain is a process. The process gets easier when we purposefully replace the self-destructive chatter in our head with positive thoughts.

Forgiveness is rarely a one-time shot. It takes daily practice. Don't give up and you will experience healing over time.

Forgiveness is a great idea because it was God's idea..

God began by forgiving us. He invites us to forgive others. Your willingness to participate in the process of forgiveness is a measure of just how much you appreciate being forgiven by God.

More Forgiveness For The Soul?

Most of the stories you have read in this book were submitted by readers like you who were interested in sharing their experiences. We will be publishing at least two Forgiveness for the Soul books every year. We invite you to contribute a story to one of these future volumes.

Stories may be up to twelve hundred words and must uplift or inspire. You may submit an original piece or something you have read.

To obtain a copy if our submission guidelines and a listing of upcoming Forgiveness books, please write, email or check our Web site.

Please send your submissions to:

Forgiveness For The Soul
Web site: *www.forgivenessforthesoul.com*
P.O. Box 496, Antioch, IL 60002
Email: forgiveness@queenpublications.com

We will be sure that both you and the author are credited for your submission.

For information about speaking engagements, other books, audiotapes, workshops and training programs, please contact us at: forgiveness@queenpublications.com

Contributors

A few of the stories in this book were taken from previously published sources. These sources are acknowledged in the permissions section.

The remainder of the stories were submitted by readers who have chosen to remain anonymous.

Gilbert Palmer, on air personality and commercial voiceover artist.
He and his wife Mary Palmer are the proud grandparents of 6 beautiful children and have a Disc Jockey service that specializes in weddings receptions, church events as well as serving as Emcees. Spreading the Word of God is his passion and he has plans to attend the Dallas Theological Seminary.

J. Walsh, father of two children, lives and works in a suburb of Boston. He holds a degree in Marketing and works at a Fortune 500 company as a Marketing Manager.

Harvey Jones, father of three children, is a Counselor at a non-profit agency for at-risk youths where he specializes in guiding teens to 'choose higher'. He is determined to help as many children as possible avoid the paths he chose before turning his life over to Christ.

Roberto Garcia, currently a Software Engineer, resides in southern Oklahoma where he faithfully serves in his church. He hopes his story will inspire others to not only have a forgiving heart but to also treat others with the love of Christ no matter what their race maybe.

CONTRIBUTORS

M. Richards, husband and recent father of a little girl, who has proudly converted to Christianity. He is a Manager with a major airline and is apart of a ministry where he works with those struggling to become free from indoctrination of Islam.

Discussion Questions

1) Which forgiveness story could you relate to the most? Why?

2) Are there any events within a story which you believe are unforgivable?   Which?

3) What have you learned about the importance of forgiveness?

4) Is it difficult for you look at one's mistakes, consider their humanness and them being subject to error- when trying to forgive?

5) Do you believe it more or less difficult for men to forgive than women?

6) Unforgiveness manifested in wrath for some and in sickness for other. What other manifestations did you notice?

7) What can you do to start spreading the spirit of forgiveness?

Permissions

Adopted Twice (aka Forgiven For The Past) by Briant George. ©2005 Briant George. Used by permission of Precious Testimonies (www.precious-testimonies.com).

Being Able To Forgive Those I Hated Has Set Me Free by Mark Anthony Velez. ©2005 Mark Anthony Velez. Used by permission of Precious Testimonies (www.precious-testimonies.com).

Forgiven Sex Crime Offender by Robert Swift. ©2005 Robert Swift. Used by permission of Precious Testimonies (www.precious-testimonies.com).

Ghosts From Vietnam. Reprinted by permission of MSIA ©2006 by John-Roger (www.forgive.org).

I Don't Hate God Anymore by Jim Miller. ©2005 Jim Miller. Used by permission of Precious Testimonies (www.precious-testimonies.com).

Who Is Alethea Pascascio?

Alethea Pascascio is an author, publisher, internet radio host, and forgiveness advocate. She presents workshops on forgiveness at many establishments, including but not exclusive to: churches, libraries, prisons, and schools.

Although Ms. Pascascio is an Engineer by way of education and professional, she is taking this season to spread the timeless message of forgiveness.

She is also the host of The Forgiveness Show which originated after the origination of National Forgiveness Month, September. Join her at:
www.blogtalkradio.com/forgiveness

For Alethea's availability go to:

www.alethea.queenpublications.com
Alethea Pascascio c/o
Queen Publications
P.O. Box 496
Antioch, IL 60002
Email:
Alethea@queenpublications.com

And check out: www.forgiveness.queenpublications.com

www.ingramcontent.com/pod-product-compliance
Lightning Source LLC
Chambersburg PA
CBHW020003050426
42450CB00005B/290